Also by Smiley Blanton

LOVE
OR
PERISH

By

Smiley Blanton, M.D.

SIMON AND SCHUSTER, NEW YORK

1956

LIBRARY OF CONGRESS CATALOG CARD NUMBER: 55–11043
MANUFACTURED IN THE UNITED STATES OF AMERICA
BY KINGSPORT PRESS, INC., KINGSPORT, TENN.

ACKNOWLEDGMENTS

IN PREPARING *this book I have had the help of a creative and sensitive artist, Mr. Edward Robinson. He has helped me with the style of the book; but more than this, he has assisted me over hard places and very often helped me to simplify my scientific concepts for presentation in nontechnical terms.*

I also wish to express my deep gratitude to Mr. Richard Simon, our publisher, who came along at a time of need and, through his suggestions and faith, helped us to go ahead.

Lastly, I wish to thank my wife, Margaret Gray Blanton, who has been urging me to write this book for thirty years and whose patient faith has helped me to bring it to a successful conclusion.

SMILEY BLANTON

No case history in this book has been published without permission. In each case, names and essential facts have been disguised.

S. B.

CONTENTS

LOVE

MOST people understand love to mean simply love between the sexes. It does mean this, but also much more. On the deepest level, love is an instinctive force present in every person from birth to death. It is a profound urge to preserve and extend life by means of union with another living force, and it expresses itself through an exchange of energy that mutually strengthens and rejuvenates.

Love is born when the child rests in its mother's arms. From this beginning, love grows until it includes the love of family and friends, of school and country, and ultimately of all the world. Love also means love of self. This is an aspect often ignored, yet it is of basic importance—for without healthy self-love, one cannot love anyone else. Love also means love of God, a love that sustains us when human relationships crumble.

Love is all of one piece—from the love of mother and child to the love of sweethearts, husbands and wives, and friends. It is present, too, in the laborer's devotion to his work, in the teacher's solicitude for her pupils, in the physician's dedication to his art. All that heals, cultivates, protects, and inspires—all this is a part of love.

To say that one will perish without love does not mean that everyone without adequate love dies. Many do, for without love the will to live is often impaired to such an extent that a person's resistance is critically lowered and death follows. But most of the time, lack of love makes people depressed, anxious and without zest for life. They remain lonely and unhappy, without friends or work they care for, their life a barren treadmill, stripped of all creative action and joy.

Introduction

For more than forty years I have sat in my office and listened while people of all ages and classes told me of their hopes and fears, their likes and dislikes, and of what they considered good or bad about themselves and the world around them. I have listened while mature people tried to piece together for me the converging patterns of their troubled lives. I have listened while adolescents confided their secret resentments and anxieties, and while very small children told me by indirection where things were going wrong with them. I have listened, too, while the elderly explained where they had failed, where succeeded, and what hopes they still cherished for the future.

As I look back over the long, full years, one truth emerges clearly in my mind—the universal need for love. Whether they think they do or not, all people want love. Their spoken words may tell of other things, but the psy-

Introduction

chiatrist must listen to their unconscious voice as well. He must probe deeply into the human mind and heart, for it is his function to evaluate the buried urges that determine our lives even though we often have no conscious knowledge of them whatsoever. There he sees that people sit on the threshold of their personalities, as Robert Louis Stevenson put it, and call on the world to come and love them. They cannot survive without love: they must have it or they will perish.

For without love, we lose the will to live. Our mental and physical vitality is impaired, our resistance is lowered, and we succumb to illnesses that often prove fatal. We may escape actual death, but what remains is a meager and barren existence, emotionally so impoverished that we can only be called half alive.

The poets and the prophets have defined love and expressed many great truths about it. But the modern studies of the depths of the personality have shown for the first time the structure of this love and the reason why it is so sought after and needed by human beings. It also shows why so many people, though they wish for love and often starve for it, cannot accept it even when it is offered to them.

Love is a very complex emotion, requiring a richness of personality and a great variety of talents. It is first of all the strong feeling of attachment and dependence that one feels for one's parents. This feeling grows, widens, and changes until it develops, correctly, into the many-faceted desires and strong relationships with human beings of any age or sex. It develops also into the abstract feeling for things and

Introduction

ideas, for beauty and learning, and, finally, into a feeling for the Supreme Being.

Saint Paul describes love in the thirteenth chapter of Corinthians, one of the greatest love poems ever written:

> *Love suffereth long and is kind.*
> *Love envieth not—*
> *Seeketh not her own.*
> *Thinketh no evil,*
> *Beareth all things.*
> *Believeth all things.*
> *Hopeth all things.*
> *Love never faileth.*

Because of early experience in childhood and youth, many people have ingrained in them a concept of love which is really a distortion and a caricature. They think love means surrender of their personalities, that it means inconsistency, or that it means to be bullied, dominated, and degraded. They cherish an image of love that is selfish, cruel, and immature. Such unhappy people are so afraid of love that they become suspicious, depressed, and even angry when it is offered to them.

Even when they come to the physician for help, the attention and regard that he gives them sometimes make them fearful and resentful. Possibly because it recalls some earlier relationship that promised much and ended in bitter disappointment, they flee from the very help offered them in the physician-patient relationship.

Introduction

During my first years of practice this was a disturbing thing to me. I knew from my training that many people could not completely accept a relationship that held no hatred and which could be felt only as love. Nevertheless, it astonished me to see before my very eyes how people so desperately in need of love, whose very lives depended on finding and accepting it, shied away from even the simplest expression of understanding and sympathy.

It is a surprising experience to see people living out a pattern of hatred and resentment toward a psychiatrist just because love and understanding are offered to them. Of course, the psychiatrist is trained and disciplined to continue to give his regard and friendship to those with whom he works, regardless of their feelings toward him. He does not return hate for hate. He realizes that the feelings directed toward him, whether of love or of hatred, are only partially due to something in himself or to some act of his own. Primarily they are due to the patterns of love and hatred that have been developed in the patient's mind.

I am reminded of a simple example: A young man who came to me as a patient showed unusual anger and resentment toward me during the first interview. At the end of the hour I asked him why he disliked me so. He replied, "Doctor, I know you have done nothing to me, but you look very much like my father—and I hate the old man. I guess I hate you just because you look like him." Fortunately, this particular boy was conscious of the basis of his dislike and did not rationalize it onto some behavior of mine toward him.

These attitudes toward someone else, developed in one's

early life, are transferred not only to the therapist but unfortunately onto most of the human relationships with which a person must deal. They are the pattern of his behavior.

Must people who meet love with resentment go through life unchanged? Is the situation then hopeless for those who cannot accept love? The answer is *no*. These patterns of rejection can be changed.

It is natural to reject something that threatens one's happiness. If love has been experienced as an unhappy failure, people naturally try to avoid it. But I have seen people replace hatred with love, selfishness with kindness, when they developed insight. With assistance and encouragement their true selves have emerged.

I have grown more concerned each year of my life by the fact that so many people live such unsatisfactory lives. To them life is always a battle, or a reaction against something; rarely is it an expression of an affirmative feeling that can make for happiness. The person who is afraid of love constantly reacts against it with hatred. In new surroundings he acts as though he were in the old surroundings of his early life. He eternally puts his new wine in old bottles. His behavior may be completely unsuitable to the present, but his real self is smothered by this compulsive necessity to act as though the present were the past.

Sometimes a tendency to negative reaction causes some people to reject all suggestions, even when they would like to do what is asked of them. We see this in young children. When they are asked to come to eat, for instance, they may say "no" even though they are very hungry—a sort of revolt, however, that is not suitable as a constant reaction pattern twenty years later! On the other hand, a person may slavishly accept all suggestions, whether suitable or not, for fear of being rejected by someone. In this way he avoids the repetition of some old intolerable experience in childhood. But it is only through getting a true concept of love as it relates itself to one's own development, of finding love and restoring faith, that the real person can emerge.

What can happen to a person to make him change his habitual reaction to life so that he may have a successful future? First, there must be a deep, even if unconscious, desire to change. There must be a profound and abiding conviction that reaches down into the unconscious mind. There must be a profound, if unconscious, urge to have a new life. This very desire sets the door ajar.

In the deeper levels of the mind there are resources of power, strength and courage hardly imagined. *To each person himself is given the task of tapping these levels,* with what assistance he can muster. There are, fortunately, untold resources in each of us if we will only find and utilize them.

Sometimes the influence of an understanding person—a friend, pastor, priest, psychotherapist—is able to start this change. Sometimes just an association with a person really capable of giving and receiving love can break this circle of hatred, rejection, loneliness, suffering and disappointment.

Just now the world is passing through a revolution. It is a dangerous place. People are naturally anxious and cautious. This is to be expected and is perfectly normal. The person who is well armored for this world realizes it is a

Introduction

dangerous place and so takes proper steps to meet whatever comes with courage and intelligence. The right amount of anxiety makes us take these proper precautions against danger. As a safeguard against illness and poverty in old age, for example, we take out insurance policies. When the road is slippery, we drive slowly and with caution. But many people are sick with worry not because of real dangers but because they transfer their inner anxiety over onto the world situation. They think it is the evil of the world situation they fear, when in reality it is a personal anxiety. Their real fear is that they may lose love, or that they may not be adequate to meet life. They may be afraid of growing old. But instead of facing these fears as facts and dealing with them as realities, they transfer their fears over onto the world situation and find temporary escape and relief by rejecting the truth.

The world is indeed a dangerous place! But then it always has been and probably always will be. It is our fate and glory to face this danger and bring order out of chaos, love out of hatred. Hence, to avoid this feeling of "world tension" we must analyze our own personal fear and anxiety. Of course we must also study the actual situation in order to disentangle it from our personal anxieties. We must also learn to take the long, clear view of history. That is a first step in overcoming our fear and anxiety over the world situation as it is at the present time.

In my own life I have lived through part of the Reconstruction period in the South; I have experienced the horror of war in World War I, lived through World War II, and have seen the development of atomic warfare. All this

Introduction

during one lifetime. Nevertheless, I am firmly convinced that the world is actually a better place than it was in my youth. People are kinder, there is less prejudice, less hatred, and there is a deeper realization that we must love our neighbor as ourselves.

True, the world is still full of tyranny and cruelty, but *good* is also organized as never before. The tyrants and dictators are even forced to use the very words that mean so much to free men—words like *freedom, democracy, peace*. Though they distort the words, yet must they use them. It is a tribute to the appeal which freedom and justice have for the world that these dictators must give lip service in the same words to the concepts developed in the free world.

This battle is a challenge. We may be grateful that a new science of human behavior has given us new methods for bringing light and self-knowledge to people everywhere —and thus infusing love into our lives. We can be sure that love is stronger than hate. We can be sure that "Eternal Eros," which is love, can overcome his immortal adversary of hatred and resentment. We must never call retreat in our war against hatred, prejudice and tyranny. We need never falter in our search for a healing love.

That is why for many years I have felt the need to write this book. I believe that it is possible to achieve an emotional change with the insight developed through books. Books can make a change in one's philosophy and attitude toward life. That is why so many books of the world are so deeply cherished.

It is in this hope that I write, in an effort to bring to peo-

Introduction

ple the hard-won truths of my observation over many years of life and during more than forty years of practice in psychiatry. Many people need personal counseling; but it is a fact that many can and do bring changes into their own lives through books. They can acquire not only self-knowledge but also a new concept of love; they can tap the hidden resources of the deeper mind, where there is strength and courage. For we must love—or perish.

S. B.

CHAPTER ONE

The Guardian of Life

Whatever you do in life, do with love! We have no alternative save to act from motives of hate—yet how doleful to make this our choice! For hate is the destroyer of life, where love is its guardian. Hate blinds our vision and warps our talents; but love releases our energies for the creative action that sustains mankind. While all human behavior springs from a mixture of both these great forces of nature, it is within our power to determine which shall prevail as we journey through life. The theme of this book is that we must tip the balance ever in favor of love if we wish to hurdle the obstacles before us on the road to normal happiness and success.

Love has reached across the ages to bind men together in an ever-widening circle of humanity. It has served to construct the essential fabric of most of the world's great religious and ethical teachings. Slowly but stubbornly over mankind's long history, it has tamed our savage nature and taught us how to transform a primitive wilderness into a cultivated garden.

To this day, nevertheless, most of us retain a skeptical view of love's efficacy as a practical approach to the problems of everyday life. We look for love in the heightened moments of courtship or marriage. We expect to encounter it in a mother's appealing relationship with her infant child. Experience shows us that at times of crisis it may inspire us to deeds of heroism and self-sacrifice. But men and women ordinarily dwell on far less lofty a plane, and secretly we too often despair of love's emergence except at the historic peaks of human endeavor.

The world's harsh realities would seem to justify such cynicism. None can deny that men are still largely ruled by their uglier passions, and we may be forgiven if we insist that love must be regarded chiefly as a form of idealistic aspiration—or at best as an emotional prize that falls to us only when good fortune so decrees. Yet it is my hope as a psychiatrist to show in these pages that love must be embraced in every phase of our daily lives, if for none other than reasons of enlightened self-interest. Far from being a tenuous ideal, love is a dynamic reality that serves as our only true protection against the disintegrating forces of nature both within ourselves and in the world outside. It must therefore be adopted not as an optional embellishment of life but as the fundamental source of human security and achievement.

To do this requires that we broaden our view of love beyond the narrow limitations imposed upon it by popular concepts. Love is not simply a turbulent romantic passion to which we periodically succumb; nor is it a kind of luxury to be reserved for special occasions, like rare wine at a holiday feast. On the contrary, true love shows itself as a harmonious attitude toward life in general. It is a steady, unflinching desire for constructive action which permeates the whole personality. Love is in this sense a basic emotional approach that we must develop in our work, in our relationships with other people, and also in our attitude toward ourselves.

Modern psychiatry teaches us that we fall ill, emotionally and physically, if we do not use love in this way to guide and control our behavior. When we cannot give and receive love freely, we become easy prey to the dread emotions of fear and resentment, of anxiety and guilt. These diverse expressions of hostility so distort our outlook that we are then unable to view life in a clear and objective manner. Fear paralyzes our natural impulses to explore and investigate, while resentment causes us to misinterpret what we see. Anxiety prevents us from accepting the normal experiences whereby we grow and develop to our full potentialities. Guilt, in turn, forces us to punish ourselves with accidents and faulty actions that lead to unnecessary frustration and defeat.

Against these hostile emotions neither laws nor logic can prevail. They hurtle us on to repeated errors despite ourselves—for love is the only true source of knowledge, and without it we lose our ability to learn and to understand. Once in the grip of hostility, we twist forward in a spiral of destructive action that envelops those around us and spreads beyond as a source of universal evil. It generates crime and encourages corruption in our personal lives. It leads to economic exploitation and social injustice. On a national and international scale, it foments the storms of political hatred that bring wars, revolutions and dictatorships.

Nothing can stop the spiral except love. If men have thus far failed to destroy one another, it is only because love has always emerged at the critical moment to act as mentor and guardian. All the precious instruments that help to preserve and ennoble life—medicine and religion, science and education, arts and crafts—all these have throughout history been the product of love alone. But more specifically, they were created by men and women whose individual lives were governed by love. The world rarely sees a Christ or a Buddha, and not all of us have the gifts of a Leonardo or a Pasteur. Yet countless legions have followed in their lead to help erect the vast edifice of love that we know as culture and civilization.

And from this we must take our cue. We need not remain mired in the unstable and neurotic patterns of hostility which waste our substance and cause us to limp along in a painful simulation of life. Nor need we wait helplessly until heroic champions rescue us from the abyss. Each of us may learn the lesson of love for himself, and with its power we can correct and fortify our lives from day to day. This is now, as it has always been, our only alternative to self-destruction. But the present nature of the times indicates that we seize it without delay.

Love or Perish

Hate Breeds Self-Defeat

Our attitudes of love and hate have a practical significance that cannot be overstressed. They affect our every
action and influence our emotions at every moment of life.

Let me illustrate by a typical example. Among my patients some years ago was a businessman who owned a large
company that manufactured machinery for the oil industry.
He had started with the firm as a salesman, then gradually
worked himself up until he obtained complete control.
Later a series of business reversals overtook him, and in a
period of emotional depression he had come to me for help.

My patient was a quiet, soft-spoken man in his late thirties, apparently of a friendly and co-operative nature. Beneath his gentle exterior, however, was a spirit of ruthless
aggression. He had won his success largely by a process of
undermining several officers of his firm. He had gone about
these maneuvers with cold and quiet determination, until
eventually the other men found themselves ousted from
positions they had held for years.

As often happens when hate and aggression are trium-
phant, my patient had then unconsciously set about to destroy with his left hand what his right had achieved. He
was not content with the success of his machinery business,
but began to make foolish speculative investments in oil
fields. Several of these proved so disastrous financially that
he almost went into bankruptcy. To cap the climax, his
confidence was betrayed by three young men whom he had
brought into his firm and placed in positions of responsi-

16

bility. They deserted to a rival company, taking with them several of his most important customers.

Setbacks of this kind occur every day in the business world and are usually attributed to "poor business judgment" or to "misplaced confidence." When my patient's past history was unraveled, however, it turned out that these faulty actions had been brought on by a deep emotional confusion within himself. As a boy he had had a basically unsatisfactory relationship with his father. The older man was an adventurous and flamboyant kind of person who conducted his business affairs somewhat in the spirit of a gambler. He was forever making and losing money in one venture after another, and these far-flung business interests had kept him constantly away from home.

My patient was an only child, and the father's extended absences had left him with the sense of being deserted most of the time. His mother, a sweet and gentle person, quietly put up with her husband's unpredictable ways. But she came to rely more and more on her son as an outlet, and the boy grew up with a constant awareness of the undue emotional burden thus placed upon him. His reaction to this family situation was an equivocal one. At times he was filled with secret admiration for his father's adventurous activities and yearned to emulate him. More often, he harbored a deep resentment because he felt the older man had denied him the normal love and companionship other boys received as a matter of routine.

Now the thread of connection between love and life is a subtle one, often difficult to trace. It winds its way for the most part in the submerged layers of our unconscious mind, and usually we are unaware of the precise points at which it may become snarled or broken.

Yet almost invariably it is in childhood that the path of love goes astray, and so it proved in the case of my patient. As we probed into his background, it became clear that his conflicting emotions toward his parents had become the model for his later conduct in the business world. He had absorbed his mother's quiet and soft-spoken manner, but in his relationships with men he reflected the confusion that had characterized his attitude toward his father. On the one hand, he gave expression to his hate and resentment by destroying his superiors and taking their place. On the other, he tried to emulate his father's speculative business pattern by means of his wildcat investments. But a sense of guilt, which had accompanied his aggressive course, interfered with his judgment and provoked the financial losses as a means of self-punishment.

In a final attempt to win back love, he had placed his trust and affection in the three young men brought into the firm as his protégés. Yet this, too, was done more as a form of penance than an expression of genuine affection. Love so based rarely endures. In this case the young men sensed the mixed motives behind their employer's patronage, and it was inevitable that they should turn on him when greater rewards beckoned elsewhere.

Men and women are constantly trapped by this circle of self-defeat arising from buried hatreds that go back to the past. One of my patients, for example, was a young woman who had ruined her marriage largely because she could not overcome her conviction of being eternally "mistreated."

The Guardian of Life

She would accuse her husband of lack of consideration for her if he went off to play golf, or if he came home from his office a half hour later than usual. If her two small children failed to obey her instructions to the letter, she would complain angrily that they did not show her "proper respect."

In reality there was no justification for these resentments. Investigation of the young woman's history revealed, instead, that as a little girl she had been virtually trained by her mother to be suspicious and hostile in her attitude toward men. This is by no means an unusual occurrence. Many women teach their daughters that "all men are brutes, and you can never trust them." Sometimes, as in the case of my patient, the precept is so deeply inculcated that it develops into a fixed attitude toward life, with a constant feeling of abuse. Obviously, no marriage has much chance of success when the relationship between husband and wife rests on such a fallacy.

Many forms of unwarranted hostility are similarly explicable only when traced back to their hidden sources. They arise from buried resentments of the past which are carried forward and misdirected against innocent persons or objects in the present. As long as we fail to examine the true origin of our hatreds, these early resentments persist as unconscious impulses that we must irresistibly obey. That is why often we cannot stop ourselves even when our actions bring disaster upon our own heads. We cannot make a realistic appraisal of the situation because we are unable to see the part played by our own emotions. Instead, we either blame others for our misfortunes or attribute them to an evil fate.

19

Love or Perish

There are times when conflict is justified by actual circumstances. When a person is attacked in ordinary life, he properly fights back with all the aggression at his command. If we are deprived of our just due, we naturally experience emotions of anger. It is almost an axiom, however, that we must look for repressed resentments of the past as the motivating force whenever a person's *pattern* of behavior is characterized by conflict and animosity. The man who chronically fails in his work, whose friendships all end in violent quarrels, or who maintains a consistently critical attitude toward others—such a person, we may be sure, has somewhere stored up a secret hate that has stifled his basic love impulses and thus prevented him from attaining normal satisfaction and achievement. To unlock these hidden chains upon our love is for every person the essence of wisdom.

The Price of Love's Denial

The human animal, though inferior in physical strength to many other creatures of land and sea, is built of remarkably tough fiber. Mankind has survived wars, epidemics and the violent fury of the elements with astonishing resiliency. It is capable of enduring enormous hardships in the daily struggle for existence. Experience shows, too, that ordinary individuals will hold onto life with grim tenacity under the most frightful conditions of mental anguish and physical pain.

Yet there are many levels of human existence, and none

20

can take pride in mere life alone. We all vary from one another in our original constitutional structure. But every living organism is endowed at birth with its specific potentialities, and these strain for ultimate fulfillment all through its span of development. A butterfly struggles to become a butterfly from the very first instant of its larval stage, and it fails of its life purpose if for any reason it does not attain that final metamorphosis. Similarly, each human being is born to become what his original potentialities decree— whether this be priest, philosopher or clown. And every life must be chalked up as at least a partial failure when it does not succeed in reaching its inherent destiny.

Love's greatest glory lies in the fact that it alone provides the strength, protection and encouragement without which full growth is impossible. We are all aware of this truth when it comes to the life of a helpless infant. Unfortunately, too many of us ignore its equal applicability to humanity as a whole. Since men and women rarely die before our eyes for lack of love, we assume that they can live well enough without it. We do not stop to think that it is a form of death when we crawl through our days in the constant shadow of talent needlessly thwarted, of cruelties gratuitously imposed, of opportunities ruthlessly withheld—and of all those fears, illnesses and psychological self-mutilations to which we resort when hate chokes off our normal outlets of development.

If we open our eyes and look about us, we will see evidence on every hand of the price we pay when love is denied. Vivid examples exist everywhere of the kind I once witnessed in the case of a girl of eight who came to me briefly for treatment because of her inability to read. I had known the child slightly when she was two years old and remembered her as a bright and remarkably affectionate little girl. She had a wonderfully sunny disposition and would throw her arms around you gleefully at the slightest encouragement.

At the age of three, however, the child's life underwent a radical change as a result of her parents' separation. Intense friction had developed after her father returned from overseas service in the army, and the marriage was broken up after an ugly divorce action. The mother retained custody of the little girl only after a bitter court fight, and her subsequent behavior indicated that she used the child as a pawn to gain financial advantages.

A steady deterioration in the child's home life ensued. Although the mother was an intelligent woman who had once shown gifts as a concert singer, she now lapsed into a careless and disorganized kind of life. She grew rather hysterical in her general behavior and took to drinking quite heavily. The little girl was left mostly in charge of nursery schools during the day. When she returned home, she would be met either with a barrage of screaming or she would find her mother in a drunken semistupor.

One night the little girl was awakened by thick smoke in the apartment. She ran into the living room to find a cigarette hole smoldering in the arm of the easy chair. Her mother was sitting bolt upright in the chair, fast asleep with a bottle of whisky at her side. The terrified child shouted and tugged at the unconscious woman for several minutes with no effect. She finally managed to rouse her, and together they extinguished the fire.

The Guardian of Life

Similar incidents followed, usually in the form of a meal burning up on the kitchen stove after the mother had fallen asleep over her glass. The child developed regular nightmares as a result. She would wake up screaming that she smelled smoke, and run through the house calling for her mother. Whenever she saw glasses set out, she would grow panicky and beg, "Don't drink that sleepy stuff, Mommy! Don't drink it, please!"

It was only after she developed an abnormal block in reading that her teachers were able to prevail upon the mother to seek help. When the child was brought to my office, I was unable to recognize her as the little girl I once knew. She had a wild, feverish glitter in her eye. She could not sit still for an instant, but jumped and darted about the room aimlessly. When the mother insisted that she try to read something for me, the child glanced at the proffered page with a clouded and vacant expression. She mumbled a syllable or two, and all the time kept twitching her legs or scratching her arms and body nervously.

"You see!" exclaimed the mother, treating it rather as if it were a joke. "No matter what they do to her, she simply can't learn to read!"

The child involuntarily ducked her head half into her shoulder, almost as if she were avoiding a physical blow. Then she suddenly held out a bracelet on her arm for my inspection, explaining rapidly that it was one of the gifts she had recently received for her birthday. There was something quite pitiful about this frantic effort to distract our attention.

The reading problem proved to be only one of the child's

23

disturbing symptoms. She had also become something of a daredevil among her playmates, causing concern even to the neighbors. Often she would challenge her companions to dangerous feats on back fire escapes, where she liked to balance herself precariously on the railings several stories above the ground. On one of these occasions, I later learned, the frightened mother of a playmate scolded her severely and warned that she might fall and be killed. The disheveled little girl looked at her with a peculiarly glazed expression and, in a voice that had in it both defiance and wistfulness, replied, "Aw—you wouldn't care!"

In short, the once bright and endearing little girl of two had been transformed into a retarded, hostile and anxiety-ridden youngster. Before the interview was over, it became clear that the change had been largely induced by the mother's unstable and unloving attitude. She was one of those persons who outwardly observe their formal responsibilities to others but have a blind spot when it comes to the emotions of everyone except themselves. She was brittle and high-pitched, often scathing in her speech, and volubly preoccupied with her own problems and activities. Although she expressed concern about her child, her tone and manner betrayed an inner confusion tinged with hostility. She seemed to be completely unaware of the injurious effect her personal behavior was having on the little girl.

Certain human dramas occur where one can only look on in horror as the players press forward inexorably to a disastrous conclusion. This was one of them. The mother postponed our next appointment, and shortly thereafter made a characteristically impetuous decision to accept a job as administrative assistant in a Midwestern music school. In her new home the little girl was left ever more to her own devices. Playing alone with a friend one afternoon, she accepted a dare to hang by her toes from the top of a high fence—and the inevitable "accident" occurred. She lost her hold and in the subsequent fall suffered a fractured skull which proved fatal.

One may take consolation in the thought that helpful hands usually intervene to prevent stark tragedies of this kind. Not often is love altogether withheld from our lives, and ordinarily we manage to subsist even if but a few crumbs fall to our portion. Yet who can say how different might men and nations be were love more abundantly our individual lot. For lack of it, how many of us remain only half alive, stunted in mind and heart, feeble and bewildered where we could be strong and confident!

There are vast numbers whose plight is very much like that of the little girl with the reading problem. Their emotional deprivation is not so extreme, nor do they meet with a catastrophic end. But their lives are similarly burdened with needless fears and frustrations; and their personalities, too, are twisted into ugly caricatures of what they originally might have been. They constitute the discontented and rebellious among us, handicapped in turn as adults by a self-centered preoccupation with their own resentments, and driven by their insecurities to wasteful conflicts that otherwise might never have arisen.

Periodically, a dramatic revelation of love's power reminds us of how woefully we neglect this precious psychological resource as we strive to resolve the dilemmas of mankind. Such an event occurred at Panmunjom in the fall of 1953, at the close of the Korean War. The whole world marveled in amazement at that time as a handful of Indian guards, armed with nothing but walking sticks, calmed and controlled 22,000 hysterical prisoners of war who were being held in stockades while the Neutral Nations Commission conducted negotiations for their exchange.

The prisoners were Chinese and North Korean soldiers who had refused to be repatriated back to their Communist masters. They were highly wrought up, bitterly suspicious of what was going on, and for weeks their camp remained in a state of great tension. At the mere sight of a Red Chinese or Korean official, they would hurl insults or throw stones from behind their barbed-wire fences.

Responsibility for the control of this explosive situation had been placed in the hands of Major-General S. P. P. Thorat, in command of the neutral Indian guards. General Thorat, a tall and well-built man of 47 who appeared ten years younger, had won the DSO for combat service at the head of a Punjab regiment in 1945. He was an excellent athlete, a sponsor of an amateur theater company in his native India, and well known there also as a painter and art connoisseur.

General Thorat had taken a remarkable approach to his difficult task. With complete disregard for his personal safety, he had gone among the excited prisoners to explain that the Indian guards were completely neutral and wished to remain friends with everybody. He told them the guards were there to protect them and to look after their comforts and interests. Asking for their full co-operation, he assured them: "You will be happy with us."

Correspondents at the scene reported that many of the prisoners, because of language barriers, did not understand the general's words. But his meaning was unmistakably clear to them. On several occasions, his explanations had drawn bursts of applause from the captives. They had even staged a ceremony and party to which the general and his guards had been invited. As an expression of their appreciation, the prisoners fashioned a garland of colored paper flowers and presented this to the general, along with a ring hammered from a silver buckle.

For many days the patience and good humor of the Indian guards, combined with their swift and efficient action, averted one crisis after another. But on the morning of September 25 a dangerous situation broke out which threatened to end in disaster after all. The captives had learned that one of their number, a sergeant, had been released to the Communists. Instantly a wave of anger swept through the sergeant's compound, and thousands of prisoners began to riot in protest. They dragged one of the Indian officers, a major, into their enclosure and announced that he would be held as hostage until the missing captive was returned. Then, as the morning wore on, they began to rain stones upon the guards, injuring several slightly.

At this point General Thorat went to the aid of the captured major. Despite warnings that the prisoners were in an uncontrollable state, he walked into their compound accompanied only by twelve of his men, still carrying nothing but their walking sticks. One of his men spied the major, who was being dragged into a tent, and ran to his rescue—only to be captured himself. The enraged prisoners then armed themselves with tent poles and started to attack the remainder of General Thorat's party.

It was an ugly impasse. Outside, anxious officials summoned Indian troops armed with rifles and ordered them to surround the compound. As the troops made ready to fire, however, the flame of protest leaped to the other stockades and now the rest of the prisoners of war began to riot in turn. They numbered almost 20,000, and it appeared certain they would storm their barbed-wire fences to overrun the Indians altogether.

In the larger sense, General Thorat had but two alternatives from which to choose at that terrible moment—love or hate. There was ample justification for either. One view would see an army of harassed men penned in like animals, long oppressed by indignities and treacheries. In the other view, they would be simply a menacing mob, bent on murder. Yet the one might avert a dreadful catastrophe. There was no doubt that the other would cause many men to perish.

General Thorat turned to the nearest prisoner of war.

"What sort of Chinese are you?" he said quietly. "Where is your hospitality? You have offered my men neither tea nor cigarettes."

There was a moment of hesitation. Then the Chinese slowly dropped their makeshift weapons. One after another, they brought out cigarettes and offered them silently to the general and his men.

The Guardian of Life

The riot was over. Within a few minutes a committee had been chosen to represent the prisoners, and they sat down to a long and polite discussion with the general. When they learned that the sergeant had been repatriated at his own request, they decided to write an application to the Neutral Nations Commission for his return. The two Indian hostages were then freed, and General Thorat and his men were escorted by a guard of honor to the gate.

The issue between life and death is rarely drawn to so fine a point of balance as it was on that historic morning in Korea. Our lives consist rather of a series of little crises in which often there seems to be nothing more at stake than a moment of happiness. Yet always, underneath, lies the same fundamental issue. In every case we must make the same decision between love and hate, and our ultimate success or failure will depend on the basic pattern we establish. Each act we perform from motives of love pours strength and health into the stream of life. Hate causes us to perish —sometimes in a series of little deaths, sometimes at once. If we would preserve life in its fullest sense, we must choose the course of love.

CHAPTER TWO

The Immortal Rivals

W<small>E LIVE</small> in an age of atomic power when the once rhetorical question of mankind's survival has become the overriding issue in world affairs.

Each day the answer is sought by governments everywhere as nations test out political and military measures designed to ward off the catastrophe we all fear. Yet the decisive reply will not come from the official chancelleries of East or West. For the real danger now before us is not the thermonuclear bomb, any more than in former times it was the sword or the bow and arrow or gunpowder. What we basically fear today, as always, is the destructive impulses that lie within our own hearts. In the final analysis, our present emergency will be successfully met only if individual men and women in sufficient numbers the world over will once again use love to conquer hate in their personal lives.

I believe that we will meet this crisis and solve it. Humanity has undergone many periods of severe strain comparable to our own, and even worse. The religious wars in the seventeenth century reduced the population of Germany from 30,000,000 to 4,000,000. The Napoleonic wars tore Europe to pieces, cutting a wide swath of fear and havoc across the entire Continent. The bubonic plague—the "black death" which swept over a large part of the world in the fourteenth century—killed an estimated 23,000,000 people in Europe alone, and for a time threatened to wipe out civilization altogether. Yet mankind has repeatedly recovered from such catastrophes and gone on to new peaks of co-operative achievement.

From the record of the past, one derives the impression, in fact, that men have never been free of mortal threat from psychological as well as physical dangers. The history of their struggles shows a constant flux forward and back— from health to sickness, from peace to war, from achievement to destruction. The philosopher Schopenhauer likened mankind to a herd of porcupines huddling together to keep warm. If they draw too close, they prick each other painfully with their needles; if they separate too far, they freeze. Only by constant shifting about can they determine just what position will avoid both extremes.

Now it is true that our contemporary crisis allows us less margin for error than ever before. The incredibly destructive power of modern weapons makes each false step a major threat to our existence, and there is an unprecedented urgency in the need for effective solutions to our problems. Nevertheless, it is also true that the greater the danger, the stronger the defense it evokes. We command unsuspected reservoirs of strength when life itself is placed in jeopardy.

Love or Perish

I recall a striking confirmation of this fact which occurred many years ago in the schizophrenic ward of a hospital where I was a staff member. One of the patients there was a young man who was completely psychotic in his behavior. He was altogether lost to reality: he babbled incoherently in conversation, and his symptoms included extreme hallucinations like seeing monstrous bears in the clouds outside his window. In a fit of frenzy, this patient one day plunged the broken-off handle of a tooth brush into his own chest. The wound became infected and the young man developed an acute case of lobar pneumonia, with dangerously high temperatures.

At this point, to everyone's surprise, he suddenly became completely rational. For two weeks he remained a perfectly "normal" person, fully aware of all that happened around him. He discussed current matters with us, including his illness, in a wholly sensible manner, and was even able to take a clear view of his schizophrenic behavior, which he himself called strange and abnormal. Such mental recoveries, however, rarely last. Once the young man had been pronounced safely out of danger from the pneumonia, he lapsed back into his psychotic state as completely as he had come out of it.

Many psychiatrists can cite similar cases in their clinical experience. The mystery of these temporary recoveries is explained by the fact that the life force within all of us comes to our aid whenever a true emergency arises. Our unconscious mind, if it is confronted with a real danger in the objective world, gives up its fantasies in order to fight the actual threat to one's life. While this manifests itself in psychotics as an extreme contrast to their usual behavior, it is of course an everyday part of the normal person's psychology.

Our great concern today is whether we can afford to wait until the last moment of peril before we bring this psychological mechanism into play. Although we may be confident that it will automatically emerge in time to forestall a major holocaust, mankind meantime lives under a terrible burden of unhappiness. We not only must shoulder the overwhelming material costs of armed preparedness, but also suffer psychological anxieties that drain our energies almost to the breaking point. If we wish to make life something more than a matter of mere physical survival, therefore, we must seek at once to control our own destructive fantasies which lie at the root of the problem.

Psychiatry teaches us that destructive fantasies arise when our need for love is unduly thwarted. We operate on an internal emotional economy in which conflicting primitive drives maneuver constantly for dominance. This restless emotional battle is fought by each individual within himself, and is brought under control only when love assumes command.

But every acquisition of external power over nature disrupts our inner psychic adjustment in so far as it increases our destructive capacity. That is the heart of modern man's dilemma. The conquest of the atom has made it imperative that once again we conquer ourselves. We have reached one of those historic moments in the evolution of mankind when a new surge of love must flow forth to counteract a new riptide of hate.

Love or Perish

Balance

It will help us to gain a deeper concept of love if we will look for a moment at the essential nature of life itself. Biologists are agreed that all living organisms show one great path in common—whether it be a lizard or a tree, an amoeba or a human being. Life in every instance is essentially the force that *combines* individual atoms and cells, *builds* them into the pattern of the organism's destined structure, and then heroically *holds together* what has already been built.

The initial impulse to combine and build is perhaps most dramatically illustrated in the power that lies hidden within the seed. Frail and negligible as it may at first appear, the tiny seed has within itself the miraculous secret mechanism that knows how to put together water and oxygen, carbon and sulphur, and all the other things that will mature into a plant, a flower or a tree.

This mechanism is fantastically persistent in reaching toward its final goal. A pine tree has a characteristic shape, for example, with each of its predestined number of branches shorter than the one below. If the lowest branch is artificially destroyed during the growing process, the tree starts all over again. It puts forth a new lowest branch of the same length, then continues on with its design as before. The same type of dogged persistence is shown by a sunflower when it happens to take root on the shady side of a barn. It will curve around the corner of the building in order to reach the sunlight it craves for its growth.

The Immortal Rivals

Nature presents many other striking examples of the remarkable tenacity with which living organisms hold themselves together, once their structure has been developed. This is shown clearly in the case of the sponge, which is one of the simplest forms of animal life. A sponge consists of four different kinds of cells. Experiments have been conducted in which these are artificially broken up by pulling the sponge apart and even squeezing it through a silk cloth. Provided they have not been individually injured in the process, these disorganized cells will regroup themselves in proper positions and produce a whole animal again!

At every stage the living structure concentrates on its primary task, which is to preserve itself and to follow out its allotted course. Physiology tells us that this can be successfully accomplished *only if the living organism is able to maintain the internal balance by which it holds itself together.* A counterforce—in the form of tensions, pressures and chemical changes both within and without the organism — constantly upsets this internal balance, and thereby threatens to destroy the structure as a whole. But the instinctual force of life, which works through a marvelous regulatory mechanism, opposes these destructive tendencies by restoring and maintaining the original balance.

Every living thing has its own state of equilibrium peculiar and proper to itself. In plants, for example, the sap in the cells of a given tissue requires a certain hydrogen-ion concentration, or acidity. The plant must be able to maintain this level of acid concentration in order to live, and it does so despite constant changes in the external environment.

Love or Perish

Man has his own characteristic state of internal balance, for which the distinguished Harvard biologist, William B. Cannon, has proposed the term "homeostasis." This balance within the human body is a marvelously delicate business. It embraces the glandular system, with its secretion of hormones, enzymes and vitamins, and it involves constant psychic and chemical reactions of infinite complexity.

One example of this regulatory mechanism is the process by which we maintain our body temperature at a steady level despite outside changes of heat and cold. Another is the series of chemical reactions by which the proper concentration of sugar and glycogen is maintained within the circulatory system. If too much sugar is present, it is automatically transformed into glycogen, the form in which carbohydrates are stored. When the sugar concentration is too low, the process is reversed and stored glycogen is transformed back into the amounts of sugar necessary to achieve proper equilibrium. Disease develops when these processes break down so that a permanent imbalance results. Diabetes occurs, for example, when the reversible sugar-glycogen reaction fails to take place.

Most of these reactions, of course, occur on an automatic level. Occasionally we have visible evidence of this unconscious mechanism, such as the rapid breathing that takes place after strenuous exertion. Here it is the excess carbon dioxide in the blood which automatically increases the rate of the heartbeat and lung action until the deficient supply of oxygen is restored. Perhaps the most primitive example of all is the universal phenomenon of hunger pangs, due to contractions of the stomach, which warn the body to replenish its depleted supply of food.

The ultimate source of the homeostatic process remains pretty much of a mystery. But its basic functional significance is perfectly clear. As the American biologists, Young and Stebbins, put it: "So much of the body's activity can be seen to center around maintaining a balance of concentration among the substances in the blood that the physiologist is almost tempted to view the maintenance of this equilibrium as the central purpose of life."

In biological terms, then, every living organism is characterized by a ceaseless struggle between two great opposing forces. One force seeks to upset the organism's internal equilibrium. If it succeeds, it produces a state of disorganization that results first in disease and finally in total destruction or death.

The other force battles to restore the original state. As long as this force triumphs, it will maintain the proper balance and thus preserve life. It follows that the health of an organism at any given point will depend on the relative strength of the two opposing forces as they clash in their eternal struggle.

Eternal Eros

One of the most fascinating aspects of modern psychoanalytic research has been its demonstration of the remarkable parallelism between our emotional life and these fun-

37

damental biological processes. In probing the origin of emotional illness, Sigmund Freud discovered that human beings are motivated by two basic instinctual drives. One embraces the powerful forces of love, or *Eros;* the other comprises the relentless forces of aggression, or hate. It is in the mutual interreactions of these great instinctual streams of energy that Freud found the explanation of man's emotional behavior and development.

Love, in our psychic life, is the great combining force *that seeks to join all parts together.* It is the organizing element in our emotional structure. It is the power that reaches out to build and construct. Love is the immortal flow of energy that *nourishes, extends and preserves.* Its eternal goal is life.

Side by side with it there exists the antagonistic force of aggression. This is the dark instinct that strives constantly *to pull the parts asunder.* It it the power that conquers and dissolves. It bores inward, seeking to separate and destroy. Aggression's goal is death.

From the very beginning of our lives, the two primitive drives of love and aggression meet and become inextricably entangled with each other. Each of these forces is an indispensable source of energy, and human life would be impossible if either were to be eliminated. Man's great task is to maintain in his psychic life, as in the biological, what one might call an "emotional homeostasis." That is to say, we must achieve a steady balance of the opposing instinctual forces in order to maintain a proper functioning of our psychological structure. If we lack sufficient aggression, we will be unable to command the basic strength necessary to carry out the daily tasks of life. On the other hand, if love is weakened in its drive or arrested in its expression, the opposing force of aggression will overflow its proper channels and dangerously corrode the sustaining walls of our psychic organization, even to the point of death.

No one who has ever brought up a child can doubt for a moment that love is literally the life-giving fluid of human existence. Tragic proof of this fact has been dramatically provided in a documentary film made some years ago by the American psychoanalyst, Dr. René A. Spitz, in a South American foundling home. The film tells the pitiful story of a group of ninety-seven babies, ranging in age from three months to three years, who sickened and died for lack of love.

These infants were in the ordinary sense neither neglected nor abused. The orphanage in which they had been placed was equipped to give normal routine care. The children were adequately fed, clothed, and given proper medical attention. Competent nurses ministered to their daily physical needs. Only one element was lacking. The institution was badly understaffed, and each nurse had to care for ten or more of the helpless orphans. The burden of this daily regimen was so great that the nurses could do little more than feed, clothe and bathe the children. They had no time to play with their charges; they could give them no comfort or emotional exchange of any kind. A malignant fate dictated that for the greater part of each day these infants were left by themselves, to live in stark loneliness.

A sorrowful development now ensued in that remote South American scene. The deprived infants at first reacted to the loss of their parents by showing little more than a demanding attitude and an increased tendency to cry. But within three months grave symptoms of abnormality became painfully apparent. The children lost their appetites, were unable to sleep, and showed a mournful vacancy of expression in their eyes.

At the end of five months, deterioration had set in with accelerated swiftness. Most of the babies became shrunken beyond recognition. They lay whimpering and trembling, their faces twisted into grotesque expressions. The film has one harrowing sequence in which the doctor tries to comfort a fifteen-month-old girl. He picks her up gently and smiles. But the child screams in panic. One hand clutches the doctor for protection; the other beats wildly at him in terror. In the child's agonized countenance one recognizes the horrifying features of a person driven insane by loneliness and fear.

Twenty-seven of those children died in their first year of life. Seven more died in the second year. Another twenty-one who remained in the institution managed to survive, but they were so altered by the experience that they had to be classified as hopeless neurotics, or worse. Lack of normal love had laid waste the lives, in all, of more than half the original group of infants.

From so grievous a tale one turns in sadness, yet with the clear realization that denial of love may in truth prove as lethal in its consequences as the most virulent disease. Its effects may not strike adults with the same concentrated impact, but the eventual result may be no less devastating. The fact is that our emotional health at any given point de-

The Immortal Rivals

pends on the degree of balance achieved between love and aggression. If there is a prolonged dislocation of the normal equilibrium between the two, fear and tension are created and a major disease may follow.

Recently the Canadian research physiologist, Dr. Hans Selye, has shown that stress may produce almost any disease by its effect on the body's hormonal output. Our internal chemical balance is controlled mainly by the pituitary and adrenal glands. Stress of any kind, whether physical or emotional, creates an "alarm reaction" which causes these glands to pour out excess hormones. The purpose is to correct chemical imbalance; but if the alarm reaction remains chronic, the glands become exhausted and resistance to disease is thereby lowered. Proper utilization of sugar is also affected, with a consequent loss of energy. Such conditions, Dr. Selye found in his experiments, lead to the development of illnesses that range from hypertension and arthritis to rheumatic fever and heart disease.

These laboratory findings merely confirm what we may observe with our own eyes in everyday life. A year and a half ago, for example, I was consulted by a young woman who had just broken her engagement because the man she had loved proved to be a domineering person with whom it was impossible to get along. She was a woman of about twenty-five, but when she came to see me she appeared at least ten years older. Her face was haggard and drawn, her skin looked dead, her hair was without luster.

I saw her again about six months later, when she had fallen in love with another man of admirable qualities whom she was about to marry. Now her face shone brightly, her eyes sparkled, and her skin was aglow. Clearly, her earlier frustration had depressed her body metabolism, and especially the glands of internal secretion. When I saw her the second time, love and happiness had quickened the metabolism again and restored her natural vitality.

It should be remembered, however, that physical illness is only one form of reaction to disturbances in our psychic economy. As Dante observed, "It is love that spins the universe," and all life suffers when we fail to use love properly. Love plays a vital role in the way we rear our children, in the work we perform, in our daily relationships with other people, and in the larger arena of public affairs. For each of these spheres represents a complex structure of human relationships, and love, as we have seen, is the primary force that holds all living organisms together.

More than bodily health is disrupted, therefore, when love goes astray. We destroy our careers, ruin our marriages, impose intolerable burdens of frustration or despair upon ourselves and those around us. Juvenile delinquency and adult crime are social products of emotional imbalance, as are also such widespread afflictions as alcoholism and narcotic addiction. And at the end of the ruinous cycle is the intransigence of nations which leads to open warfare and actual destruction.

These psychological ailments exact an infinitely greater toll of unhappiness than perhaps all our physical diseases combined. They leave us without a true purpose to inspire our actions, so that life becomes little more than a dusty scuffle across a parched terrain leading to the grave. To balance love and aggression within our natures is therefore the most urgent task before all of us, and in subsequent pages I shall try to show how this can be accomplished. For a proper balance is the only remedy which goes to the very source of the evil. It is the key to life itself, and hence the one victory we must gain in order to assure all others.

The Utopian Error

If love is a basic instinctive force, like hunger or thirst, one may well ask the question: What need is there for instruction in it? The plant pollinates and grows without visible guidance; the salmon spawns and seeks its natural habitat without external aid. Can we not trust so powerful an instinct as love to function efficiently in man, too, if left to operate by itself?

The answer to this question will be found in the basic fact that human beings start life with a greater need for love than perhaps any other living creature. The human infant is born utterly helpless and is dependent upon the love and protection of others for its very survival. He quickly learns that love is the indispensable element of his life, and that the threat of its loss is literally the greatest danger he can face. The child tries to guard against this peril by developing reaction and behavior patterns which will tend to insure the indispensable supply of love from his protectors. It is here that the archetype of all our later love patterns is established.

All through life we remain group-living creatures whose

individual welfare depends to a considerable extent on the love relationships we set up with other persons. But our mature behavior in this respect is powerfully influenced by our experience in the original infantile and childhood situation. In other words, the adult's pattern of success or failure in establishing satisfactory love relationships is something that he has *learned* in his early past. We are born only with the *need* for love; it is our early experience which teaches us *how* to love.

If all of us were automatically versed in the correct way to impart and absorb the lessons of love, our later success might be largely assured. But life surrounds us with a bewilderingly complex web of circumstance. Even the wisest among us are often perplexed by the welter of conflicting views and desires, and it is not strange that errors should creep in, especially in childhood. We unconsciously expect so much of love, in those early years, that our reactions easily veer to false extremes when we do not obtain it in exactly the way we wish.

One of the major errors with which we must cope is the assumption that love will banish strife and frustration forever from our lives. This is an idealistic concept which can never be fulfilled. It leads us to false expectations in our personal relationships with others, and sets up impossible social goals—for example, the dream of "lasting peace" among men and nations. When disappointment inevitably overtakes these expectations, we decide there is no alternative but to turn away in bitterness and condemn love itself as an illusion.

The Immortal Rivals

This is precisely the pattern of behavior commonly followed by the neurotic person. One of my patients, for example, was a man of thirty-five who had been an instructor in a Midwestern college. For years he dreamed of a post in an Eastern university which represented for him the ideal of culture and intellectual superiority. An opening finally occurred, and he was asked at what salary he would wish to start. Now had he been realistic in his expectations, he would have arranged for a personal interview during which he could have worked out a satisfactory compromise if necessary. Instead he wrote back, stating a sum which proved to be several hundred dollars more than the Eastern university was prepared to pay. They replied that they could not meet his terms, and withdrew the offer.

The instructor was utterly crushed. He reacted as if all life had been ruined by the collapse of his dream, and he fell into a depression which lasted for months. Angry and disillusioned, he resigned from his college post and took a job as a copy writer in a Chicago advertising agency. He was basically unsuited for this work, but in his bitterness he refused to go back to the profession he had so foolishly abandoned. When he came to see me, some time later, he was a man without a true purpose in life, and miserably unhappy because of it.

Many persons possess this uncompromising trait in their character, even though it may appear only in little things. We all know people, for example, who will not attend the theater unless they get tickets for aisle seats exactly in the center, or who will refuse to join a group for dinner unless the others accept their choice of restaurant. When such an attitude is extended to important matters, as in the case of the college instructor, grave consequences ensue.

We must guard against this typically neurotic view which sees life in terms of "all or nothing." Applied to our concepts of love, and to human relationships in general, it can result only in utopian expectations that must inevitably meet with disappointment. For behind such idealism is the erroneous belief that love and aggression are mutually exclusive —that one cannot truly love if aggression also is present. Those who adopt this view misconceive the very nature of life. Specifically, they fail to distinguish between neurotic hate and the normal aggressive drives present in every healthy person.

To assume that the one must be renounced along with the other is a fundamental psychological fallacy. Love may legitimately strive to banish the unjustified hatreds and hostilities which have ever proved so disastrous to human happiness. But we endanger life itself if we think that the goal of love is also to turn men into docile creatures stripped of all aggressive energy. The truth is that our primitive drives constitute a basic source of power without which none of us could exist; indeed, our failures often occur because we have not learned how to fortify this indispensable gift of nature. Love's true purpose is not to stifle our aggressive energies, but rather to employ them in the proper service of mankind.

All of us must grasp this essential distinction if we wish to cure the psychological ills that beset us in contemporary society. Mankind's real problem is not aggression itself. The sickness from which the world suffers is rather the unconscious fear and guilt aroused by mistaken attitudes toward our own aggression. It is this guilt which corrupts our lives —for the guilt is transformed into neurotic hate, and the hate in turn gives rise to the destructive fantasies that drive us forward to irrational action.

A true concept of love, then, is one which will teach us to accept our own aggressive impulses as a normal part of life. It will show us how to turn these into constructive action; and in this way love will free us from a sense of guilt. We will then seek not so much to become "peaceful" citizens because of idealistic scruples, but will strive rather to be *productive* men and women—and hence peaceful because free of any need to develop neurotic forms of hostility.

Such a concept of love will also help free us from the cruel tensions and anxieties of our time. We experience these tensions because our mistaken view of aggression causes us to turn harshly upon ourselves with excessively severe standards that cannot be met. And the person who is severe with himself will be severe with others. Love, especially normal self-love—which is so necessary for our health—helps us to avoid self-criticism. It leads us to take a more kindly view of ourselves, and therefore of our fellow men as well. This balance of outgoing love and self-love, with the absence of guilt, enables us to understand the lesson implicit in Christ's simple definition: "God is love."

CHAPTER THREE

The Miracle of Man and Woman

O<small>F ALL</small> nature's devices for achieving balance among the forces of life, surely none is a more wonderful creation than the division of mankind into male and female. Long association has led us to accept the differentiation of the sexes as a commonplace axiom of all existence. But familiar things are often the most mysterious; and the phenomenon of man and woman, like the sky and the water, is no less a miracle because it is presented to us every day. One need only imagine its absence to become acutely aware of the overwhelming grandeur with which it carries out nature's basic design.

For it is in the joyful union of a man with a woman that the jangled forces of life fall at last into harmony. Here, in the eternal longing of one to join with the other, we may discern an infinite wisdom distilled from billions of years of patient evolution. Here lies the primordial pattern of all our striving and all our bliss. It is the secret spring that animates our deepest desires and shapes our loftiest dreams. It generates the restless tension, the driving energy, that ever moves us to aspire and to achieve. From its profound yearning comes all creation, whether of the body or of the spirit. And in its successful culmination is the prototype of all our victories. Man and woman, united in loving endeavor, truly encompass the sum and substance of human life.

Viewing this marvel of nature, one would expect man and woman to give thanks each day that the other exists. Yet what turmoil, what antagonism, surrounds the love that should bring them happily together! How often do they use it, instead, as an instrument to torment each other and even to strike each other down! We need not read the mournful statistics of the divorce court to learn that love may be, in the words of Euripides, "the sweetest thing in the world . . . and the bitterest." We have only to use our eyes to see how on every hand the waves of love are trailed by a seething foam of anguish and despair. It would almost seem, to judge by reality, as if enduring love were no miracle to cherish at all, but a mere fantasy born of romantic idealism and largely doomed to heartbreak and disillusion.

One cannot deny that love and marriage too often fail in the end to bring their original promise of happiness. But to what extent is this toll of shattered dreams truly inevitable? Like so many other disillusions, may not this one, too, be the payment exacted for false expectations? If so many of our defeats are due, as we have observed, to erroneous emotional attitudes, it may be that here, again, we misconceive the true meaning of nature's design. At bottom, perhaps it is not love and marriage, but we ourselves who are the real betrayers.

Love or Perish

Certainly it is true that love between men and women has throughout human history been viewed in endless guises, according to the eye of the beholder. Men have conceived of love as a conquest to be imposed, a snare to be set, or a duty that one may command. Some view it as an adornment, like a flower to be added to life's decor. Others see it as a fruit to be plucked and devoured. Still others have interpreted love as a prize that must be captured, or a tribute that one may exact.

Countless hosts have struggled and died clutching such precepts grimly to heart. Yet all of these views have one great error in common. They conceive of love as something apart, as if it were a special entity that could survive or perish by itself, without relationship to everyday life. They turn love into a garment that may be worn or not at will, as the fancy strikes or as opportunity affords.

In the deepest sense, love is none of these things. It is not a commodity or an isolated phenomenon. True love is a continuing process, a basic way of life. It must pervade one's entire personality and infuse every action with its creative beneficence. It must well up from the depths of one's character, or it will not flow at all.

True love between two people, in its essence, is a free process of *exchange*. It is, above all, an exchange of energy. When people truly love they "give of themselves" in a literal sense, investing each other with a psychic energy that strengthens and invigorates. In the sexual exchange, the flow of energy is transmitted in its basic form. But around this develops a multitude of additional expressions: attention and care, understanding and confidence, encouragement and inspiration. These are dynamic forces which nourish the spirit as powerfully as bread and water sustain the body. It is their continuing and mutual exchange that distinguishes love in its truest form—the love, in short, that supports life and renews it each day.

Escape from Self

To take such a view of love is to spin no romantic web of the imagination. Neither is it to saddle love with arbitrary moral or ethical concepts. It is a realistic definition based, rather, on biological truths that lie at the heart of all manifestations of life throughout the universe.

It takes its cue from two remarkable facts long known to scientific investigators. The first is drawn from studies of the simpler forms of life. It shows that *a single cell, if left to function by itself, quickly degenerates and dies.*

The second fact is derived from observations of the higher forms of life. It shows that *the union of different cells into more complex organisms has been nature's way of prolonging their span of life.*

What happens when groups of cells combine into a complex structure is that each cell takes on more than one duty. The individual cell is no longer concerned simply with its own survival, but must serve to help the other cells function as well. It sends part of its energy to its neighbors, who give back part of their own energy in turn. In this way, all of them are strengthened far beyond their original powers, and the whole organism develops a durability that none of its individual parts possess by themselves.

A simple illustration from everyday life will indicate how this mechanism works in human beings. When a finger is cut, for example, the cells in the skin and flesh around the wound are more or less severely damaged. Through the nervous system, the rest of the body is notified of the emergency, and immediately the proper measures are taken to repair the injured cells. The blood rushes antibodies to combat possible infection from invading bacteria. Other organs of the body send additional substances required for healing purposes. By co-operative action of the rest of the body, in short, the injured cells in the finger are restored to their original, intact state.

But the "doctrine of mutual aid" extends even beyond such immediate requirements. From the process of union, as we know, higher organisms also achieve a form of immortality. They do not survive in their original state, but a reproductive cell separates from the parent organism and creates new life by joining with another reproductive cell. One aspect of this process is especially significant. As Freud pointed out, "the reproductive cell is fortified for this function, or only becomes capable of it, by the mingling with another like it and yet different from it."

Scientists have further shown that one cell has a rejuvenating influence upon another even without actual union of the two. Lorande L. Woodruff, the Yale University biologist, proved this early in the century by a remarkable series of experiments performed on protozoa (single-celled animalcules that reproduce by self-division). He found that a protozoon will perpetuate itself indefinitely *as long as new substances are introduced into the nutrient fluid in which it is placed to live*. The protozoon grows feeble and dies, Woodruff discovered, when it is permitted to remain in the unchanged waste products of its own metabolic processes. To put it another way, the protozoon is the cause of its own death as long as it is left alone.

But the whole picture changes the moment something new is put into its nutrient fluid. Even the introduction of waste products of a distantly related species is enough of a stimulus to maintain full vigor. By changing the nutrient fluid, in fact, Woodruff was able to trace propagation of the protozoa to more than three thousand generations. In a later experiment, he maintained a race of paramecia through more than 20,000 generations. The last descendant, it was found, remained as vigorous as the first.

Spectacular evidence of this kind in itself gives us profound insight into the nature of life's vital processes. It becomes doubly significant when coupled with the additional insight afforded by psychoanalytic research. For the study of the mind indicates quite clearly that human emotions, or feelings, are but the conscious expression of our unconscious bodily processes. All of us recognize this to be true when it comes to the feeling of pain we experience upon suffering a physical blow. But it is also true of such emotions as rage and frustration, which do not seem to have any apparent bodily origin. The whole development of psychosomatic medicine, in fact, is based on this assumption that "psychic" (emotional) states and "somatic" (bodily) illnesses are mutually interrelated.

Love or Perish

With this clue, it will be seen at once that love is not simply a poetic fancy, but a true expression of a deep unconscious experience and need. To say that love is "an exchange of psychic energy," in other words, is to state a literal fact. The woman who scans the face of her lover anxiously when he is disturbed, and reaches out with soothing hand to comfort him, is actually transmitting to him a healing force from within her own nature. She is obeying the same kind of impulse that directs the heart to pump more blood to a wounded limb. Her gift of love is but a more complex expression of the same mingling process which, on the lowest scale of life, enables one protoplasmic cell to rejuvenate another.

By a similar mechanism, obstacles which impede love's proper function will find both a bodily and an emotional expression. The man who cries out piteously that he is being "torn apart" by the conflicts of a broken home is using more than a mere figure of speech. In one such case that came to my attention, a vigorous man in his middle years suffered an apoplectic seizure during a period of estrangement from his wife in which they had lived tensely together in the same house for weeks without exchanging a word.

Love, then, is not an external accompaniment of life, but the very stuff out of which life is fashioned. In this sense, none of us is wholly without love—for we are all born with love of self. As biology reveals, it is the energy of love which constructs our body in the first place, and it is this love energy which serves thereafter to keep its numerous parts working harmoniously together. The destiny each of us faces is to turn part of our love energy outward so that we

The Miracle of Man and Woman

may be continually refreshed and strengthened for each new task in life. Alone, we can only lock this energy within the confines of our own frame, where ultimately it will consume the very bone and tissue—yes, the very soul—it thinks to preserve.

The miracle of man and woman lies precisely in the path it offers of escape from self-immolation. Love binds the two together; but in this way love is also the releasing force that frees each from self, and so enables one to preserve the other. Something of this eternal truth was glimpsed by Schopenhauer when he wrote: "Every parting gives a foretaste of death; every coming together again a foretaste of the resurrection."

Love's Twin Heritage

But there's the rub—*the destiny each of us faces is to turn part of our love energy outward!*" That is the rack on which so many of us are broken, for men and women fight this destiny even as they yearn to embrace it. Over and over again they turn their backs on the path of escape from self, though knowing in their secret hearts that such a retreat will destroy the happiness they so desperately seek. Like people with wry necks, they turn and twitch their faces toward each other, yet always remain averted.

What do they fear? One readily concedes that it is necessary to fight enemies who would destroy us. One can see a realistic justification for envy and suspicion when found

among rivals, or even for deception and cruelty when prac-
ticed by competitors. But to lacerate and repel those with
whom we would join our souls—surely, this is a weird paradox that violates one of nature's profoundest laws!

Nothing will be gained, however, by hurling epithets,
since nature itself has spun the paradox in the first place. If
human life were played out entirely on the unconscious
level of the simple cell, it might be an easy task for us to
meet and automatically bestow upon one another the love
each needs. But nature has decreed otherwise. We do not
come into the world fully formed. Nature equips us only
with the primordial seed of love, and leaves to us the task
of bringing it to fruition. Each of us must earn nature's
legacy all over again before we can claim it truly as our
own.

What a formidable, even frightening task it is! Viewing
the tiny mass of humanity that cries with such frantic protest at its birth, one marvels how any of us ever succeeds in
carrying it out. For that miniature model of mankind is a
helpless creature concerned only with its own, imperative
self. All of its fragile senses are concentrated completely on
the primitive goal of self-survival. To live at all, the infant
must devote its energies exclusively to one purpose: it must
demand and *receive* the basic necessities—food, warmth
and protection. The infant *gives* nothing. It knows no one
and nothing outside its own body. It has no duties and no
needs except to be loved and satisfied.

Up until its birth, this is the only pattern of life the infant
has known. Safe and serene within his mother's body, he has
had all his needs of hunger and love automatically fulfilled

the moment they arose. But now a series of harsh events shatters the blissful state of nirvana. He craves food and love as before, but no longer does fulfillment come automatically with desire. The mother has ceased to be present as an indivisible part of himself, and there is now a delay before she responds. The infant is left alone, waiting, with his needs unsatisfied—and at this crucial juncture he undergoes for the first time the feeling of frustration. For the first time he knows deprivation, with its mortal threat to his very existence.

Denied the substance of life, the infant now plunges into the ancient, harrowing drama destined to be played in every nursery, from palace to hovel, the world over. He screams in rage, and his whole body thrashes with the vigor of his protest. To us, as adults, this scene may appear commonplace enough. We have heard babies cry a thousand times, and it becomes a routine incident in every family household. But the experience is a new one to the infant. For him, hunger is a major catastrophe, and he reacts with primitive violence. His intense desire and uncontrollable aggression are felt as overwhelming physical sensations of pain. As he screams, he chokes and almost loses his breath. He has a profound sense of loss and devastation, and he sinks into a lonely world from which all happiness seems to have vanished forever.

The infant is rescued at last by his mother from this anguished loneliness. His clamoring needs are gratified by her, and his earlier world of joy and contentment is restored in all its heavenly peace. But the newly recovered security does not last. Hunger and desire, followed by frustration and aggression, again take possession of his body; and once more the infant is hurtled through the painful cycle of misery and bliss.

Out of this cataclysmic upheaval is born humanity's twin heritage of love and hate. Only through frustration does the infant learn that he is dependent on someone outside himself for his very life. It is the need for his mother that gives rise to his first feeling of love toward another human being. Yet he experiences this momentous event under the most distressing circumstances of fear and pain. In learning to need his mother, he has also learned that he may lose her. In learning to love and desire, he has also been filled with hatred and destructiveness.

The two opposite drives become inextricably entangled in the infant's unconscious mind. He cannot separate the desire from the fear, the love from the hate. To his primitive comprehension, it is *because* he loves—*because* he needs and desires—that he also suffers! And the suffering itself is of a dual nature. He suffers from the frustration that comes when his love is not gratified; and he suffers from the cruel agony of the hate that follows.

Clearly, this series of violent eruptions in itself now becomes a mortal danger to the infant. The furious onslaughts of love and aggression are too painful to be endured indefinitely. If he is to survive and to obtain any pleasure in life, the infant must learn to guard against the repetition of these attacks. If he is to maintain a sense of security and safety, he must somehow protect himself against both the love and the hate.

From this point on, every human being begins to devise

a lifetime series of stratagems to defend himself against the "dangers" of love. The stratagems will vary according to one's physical constitution, nervous stability, and the particular circumstances of one's environment. But in every case they will be based on our primitive response as infants to the destruction threatened by our own emotions. They will consist of compromises, disguises and alterations designed to modify the original form of our love and hate.

One infant, for example, may seek to guard against the loss of his mother's love by trying to make her again a part of himself. He will imagine in fantasy that he "eats her up," for to his primitive mind such a process of incorporation will insure his permanent possession of her. As he grows older, this type of child is likely to make impossible demands upon the people who care for him. He will be insatiable in his need for attention and love from his parents. Later on, as an adult, he may become an intolerably selfish person whom no one can bear. Such a person often fails to find any mate who can fully satisfy his exorbitant needs and desires.

Another infant may adopt an exactly opposite defense. To avoid the danger of failing to find his mother when he needs her, he may distort her image into that of a "bad" person whom he must reject. Such a child may turn away from the loved mother altogether, and later come to view perhaps all women as "betrayers." He will grow up with a permanent suspicion of all love relationships, and never be able to give anyone the full measure of his trust.

Still another child may focus his fears on the aggression that wells up within himself toward the loved mother. He may then become haunted by an eternal sense of guilt, because every person in later life who stirs his feelings of love will also arouse the accompanying incubus of aggression. As a defense, he may project these unconscious impulses of destructiveness onto others, until even the people he loves will be suspected of harboring evil and harmful intentions toward him. Or, if he retains the aggressive feelings and directs them toward himself, he may become the type of person who forever belittles his own merits. He will be the lover who abases himself and constantly proclaims his own unworthiness of love.

To some extent, of course, the mother herself influences the nature of these reactions. If she is an unstable person, for example, her sharp emotional fluctuations will intensify the infant's sense of insecurity. The mother's love relationship to the father will also have a bearing on the child's reactions. If this is not a satisfactory one, the mother may turn to the child as an emotional outlet and thereby overemphasize the mutual attachment between them. Ideally, every mother should try to develop a calm, relaxed attitude in which love and casualness are equally proportioned.

No matter how closely this ideal is approached, however, every child must experience some frustration and denial. The infant is insatiable in its demands for love, and some measure of deprivation must inevitably occur. That is why Christianity's concept of the Virgin Mother has so powerful an appeal. It fulfills the universal desire for a mother whose love knows no bounds and never falters. One easily understands why in the Middle Ages most miracles were laid to the credit of the Virgin Mother. She was conceived of as strong, fearless and helpful—an unconventional person, as Henry Adams said, who gloried in upsetting not only the laws of man but of heaven also. To this day she remains the loving person who does not threaten, as a human mother does, even those who love her. There is nothing in her love that can rearouse the sense of guilt. Moreover, there is no conflict of emotions in the surrender to her, nor any insecurity.

In real life, as we have seen, the infant views the mother's love as a source also of danger, and hence invokes various lines of defense. Few of us develop exclusively along one or the other of these directions. Our reactions are usually a mixture of the many possible stratagems, with perhaps one dominant feature emphasized above all others. Ultimately, our characters and personalities are formed by the imprint of these multiple reactions as they accumulate and repeat themselves through early life. Those reactions also set in motion the pattern of all our later relationships with others. We spend in our maturity the twin heritage of the cradle— love and hate.

The Fear of Our Memories

Looking at man's enigmatic struggle with love in the light of his infantile history, we can now see clearly wherein his salvation lies. Man's quarrel is not with love itself. His torment springs, rather, from the perilous circumstances in which love is born. What men and women fear is not love, but their memories of love! Our task of solution is therefore sharply defined. We must disentangle love from the false fantasies with which we have unwittingly surrounded it. We must learn to distinguish between the true biological and spiritual nature of love, with all its wonders, and the acquired distortions we have stored up as a barrier against it.

Our first step is to recognize the infantile period of travail as the true source of those distortions. We must understand that our early fears of love do not take place on a conscious level. They are experienced as acute bodily sensations that etch deep lines into the infant's unconscious memory. When, as adults, we take flight from love—in attacks of anxiety, of illness, of hostility or rejection or despair—we must realize that we are reviving the dim, wordless memories of infancy and attaching them, with all their nameless fears, to our mature emotions. Our course, now, must be to pierce the mists of childhood and to unravel the imagined dangers from the tapestry of the real world.

Fate has tricked us into donning those childish masks that disguise our true needs and desires. It forced us, as immature infants, to deal with vast primitive drives far beyond our little powers of comprehension. Because mankind begins life with an organism that is not fully developed, all of us were met on earth by a horde of giants whom we had to combat with an armament of pins.

As infants, our only defense was to fear. Our only tactic was to flee or, if cornered, to stand and hate. How could we know that the giants did not really exist? How could we tell that we, ourselves, would be the victims of our own attack?

The Miracle of Man and Woman

But perhaps nature had its own hidden purpose in view when it led us to this historic confusion of love with hate. We have seen that all living creatures inherit the primordial task of maintaining a state of balance between the opposing forces of life and death. Love, as we know, seeks to join all parts together and thus preserve life. Aggression, on the other hand, seeks to separate the parts and thus to destroy life. If we would fulfill our destiny, we must learn how to reconcile one with the other. May it not be that nature wished us from the very start to embark on this indispensable task of life?

The enigma of love, which couples the memory of hate within man's heart, may serve a useful purpose after all. As Freud wrote: "Nature, by making use of these twin opposites, contrives to keep love ever vigilant and fresh, so as to guard it against the hate which lurks behind it. It might be said that we owe the fairest flowers of our love life to the reaction against the hostile impulse which we divine in our breasts."

CHAPTER FOUR

Paths to Successful Marriage

I_F NATURE has decreed an eternal struggle between love and aggression, man's destiny is not merely to stand by in fatalistic fashion and let the contest run its own course. Originally, it is true, we are propelled by primitive urges like the rest of the animal world. But we are also creatures of conscious will and purpose, with the power to shape the path along which our human energies shall flow. Especially in basic relationships like marriage, where both individual and social stability are at stake, our goal must ever be to resolve the primitive conflict into a harmonious balance that serves our own best welfare.

Marriage is of course the most difficult of all our social institutions. Its success presupposes a constant process of mutual readjustment all through life, and this requires a very great degree of individual flexibility. Fortunately, nature itself provides us with certain mechanisms to help us in

64

making these adaptations. They are basic processes which all of us use to perform the daily activities of life. Ordinarily they function on an unconscious level, where they may of themselves turn aside from useful aims and thus block constructive action. Our object must be to gain a conscious control which will enable us to guide them purposefully in the direction we wish them to go.

One of the major mechanisms at our disposal derives from the inherent flexibility that characterizes mankind's basic emotional forces. Love and hate, in their original biological form, are essentially quantities of energy generated within the organism. As such, they obey a universal impulse in all living creatures: the primary objective of this energy is simply to be *discharged*—to be somehow used up so that the body's accumulated tension is released and the previous equilibrium restored.

Strictly speaking, the energy itself is indifferent to the path it is allowed to take. Nature requires only that the energy be converted into action, whether internal or external, and that it be directed toward an object—again either internal or external. Some of it must also be disposed of in typical patterns inherited over the course of human evolution. But a considerable portion of our energy is freely mobile. It does not insist on adhering to specific channels of expression. *It will accept substitute objects and alternate paths as long as it is allowed eventually to expend itself.*

Human beings, in other words, are not inevitably bound to a predestined course of action. We are not like the spider, for example, which has no choice but to use its energy for the purpose of spinning a web. A spider knows no other way to obtain food, and it must go on spinning webs as long as it lives. Similarly, a bird is driven by instinct to build its nest in a certain place every year. Even though its young may be destroyed there by marauding cats, the bird will repeatedly go back and build its nest in the same place.

For us, however, the world offers an almost infinite variety of choice. We may build houses or boats, grow potatoes or catch fish, make shoes or write poems. Our love energy may likewise be turned in many alternate directions. At the beginning of life, the infant focuses it upon himself. The energy is then turned upon the mother as the first outward love object. As life progresses, our love energy is transferred to a whole series of substitute objects. Nurse, father, teachers, companions, and, ultimately, the love partners of maturity take the place of the mother. We would never be able to establish any human relationships at all if our love were immutably chained to its original infantile path. Life as a whole may be described, in this sense, as a ceaseless search for new substitutes to replace love's original object.

The same is true of our aggressive energies. The infant's rage is directed toward anything that frustrates its desires, and the first focal point may be the mother or nurse. But this primitive impulse to destroy is later used for a great variety of purposes, many of them essential in the struggle for existence. Apart from its obvious use for self-protection against enemies, aggression provides an indispensable dynamo of energy for almost every kind of human work. The hunter kills, the woodsman chops, the cook roasts, the surgeon cuts, the lawyer prosecutes: these tasks all involve outright destruction to a greater or lesser degree. Indeed, virtually every trade or profession of civilized life entails the constant use of aggressive energy in the service of beneficent ends.

Our failures in life usually occur because this reservoir of freely mobile energy has been frozen by fear and anxiety. Thus, an outstanding trait of the neurotic person is his extraordinary *rigidity* of character. He is afraid to act freely; his emotions and behavior must always follow the same pattern no matter how harmful this may prove to be. A typical example was a patient of mine who made life miserable for her family because she always had everything planned out to the last detail. She insisted that dinner always be served at exactly the same hour, and would upbraid her husband if he were five minutes late. Every summer she went to her country home and each fall she returned to the city on precisely the same date, regardless of the weather. When she went to a party in the evening, her chauffeur always called for her at ten o'clock and she would go home whether or not she was having a good time.

In compulsive neurotics, of course, this sort of behavior takes on the intensity of a nonsensical ritual. Such persons go into a panic unless they always walk on the same side of the street, or always place their clothes in the same way on the same chair every night. Unconsciously they are afraid to give free expression to their impulses of love or aggression, and the ritual serves as a defense that prevents this.

Now there is a universally conservative tendency which leads all of us to cling to certain habits and customs. Within normal limits this is useful, for it may save unnecessary effort or protect us automatically from danger. When I returned to New York after the First World War, for example, my musette bag contained two or three candle ends, half a dozen figs and a piece of chocolate. I remember that it took me almost a week before I could empty the bag of its contents. I had so long been dependent on candlelight and emergency rations that it required a conscious effort to realize these were no longer indispensable.

A normal person will agree to change his habits or goals when circumstances demand it. If he finds he cannot get what he wants, he turns aside and tries something else. When he experiences a loss, he accepts it and goes on to the next best thing. But the neurotic characteristically cannot give things up. He holds on to childish attitudes and points of view, like a small boy who fills his pockets with junk that he will not exchange for all the treasures of the adult world. Even failure and physical suffering do not sway him from these rigid patterns. It is as if he regresses back to a more primitive level where, like the bird or spider, his behavior seems tied to instincts rather than realistic decisions.

Yet nature, as we have seen, does not impose this rigidity upon us. We cannot stop the flow of energy generated within ourselves by the portion of love and aggression with which fate endows us at birth. As long as we live, we must spend this biological inheritance in one form of action or another. But nature allows us to deflect both love and hate from their original path, and it is only our self-imposed fears which prevent us from doing so. It will help us to overcome these fears if we realize that each of us has the power to choose substitute paths which will lead to our own greatest happiness.

Paths to Successful Marriage

Maturity of Heart

A basic fear to be overcome is one we all experienced at the very beginning of life. It arises from the fact that as children we learned to encounter both love and aggression as simultaneous experiences. Since the first object of love is also the first object of aggression, there is embedded in all of us the powerful fantasy idea that the two must inevitably go together. The dual fear is like the recurrent motif of a Wagnerian opera, whose fragmented melody keeps haunting us over and over again throughout all our lives.

As adults, we must realize that the broken echo is but a fragment of the forgotten past—and not a fact of contemporary reality. We are not helpless children whose lives are completely at the mercy of superior protectors. We are no longer in the infantile position where rage is the only weapon we can use to deal with the problems of frustration or denial. Since we now know that love and aggression need not inevitably journey toward the same fixed goal, it is possible to adjust our emotions in accord with the reality of the world as we encounter it.

Our constant purpose as adults must therefore be to make sure *that we do not confuse our hate substitutes with our love choices*. It is this fatal confusion which precipitates many of the basic conflicts experienced in human relationships. Without question, it is a fundamental source of disturbance in most unsuccessful marriages.

Elsewhere, men may skip and duck through life with relative impunity, even though they fail to resolve their original

69

duality of love and hate. But marriage forces us to come to grips at last with this confused fantasy of our past. It is not like a transient episode, where men and women often turn love into a game of dream and subterfuge played for purposes of mutual deception. Marriage, by virtue of its intense reality, compels us to abandon our evasive flights into the stratagems of childhood. It demands maturity of heart, insisting that individuals deal effectively with each other on the basis of what they actually are—not as they may imagine themselves, or the other, to be. It cannot endure successfully unless it operates in the spirit described by Thomas Aquinas when he wrote: "In the living of life, every mind must face the unyielding rock of reality, of a truth that does not bend to our whim or fantasy, of the rule that measures the life and mind of a man."

The "unyielding" truth behind most failures in marriage is the fact that *love has been used as a disguised vehicle to carry hate.* The victims of an unhappy marriage rarely cite *absence* of love as the cause of their difficulties. On the contrary, when divorce occurs they almost invariably express bewilderment over what has happened. They cannot understand how two people who apparently started out with love for each other can have reached so deep a chasm of revulsion. They are genuinely perplexed by the unfathomable "change," and never suspect that their original concept of love was false from the very beginning.

All psychiatrists are consulted daily by persons whose marriages have either collapsed entirely or subsided into a permanent state of misery. The quarrels they describe and the complaints they register prove largely to be but surface symptoms of much deeper problems. Sometimes the cause of conflict is on its face a ridiculous triviality. One of my patients, a woman of middle age, resolved to seek a divorce because her husband had for years insisted on eating his meals in his shirt sleeves. In another case, a man had gone into a towering rage because his wife refused his request to hand him his golfing shoes which were nearby. The incident precipitated a vicious quarrel that lasted for weeks, and when he came to me he was on the point of breaking up his marriage.

The visible source of conflict may of course involve serious disturbances in daily life. Money disagreements, selfish behavior, interference of relatives or in-laws, infidelity, different views about the rearing of children, alcoholism— these may become tragic matters one cannot easily ignore. Yet it is also true that other people run into the same difficulties during their married lives and still manage to solve them without damage to their basic happiness.

When marriage fails, the specific complaints invariably turn out to be merely pretexts. They are masked expressions of profound psychic hostilities whose inception goes back to the hates and resentments of early childhood. Their origin is illustrated by the case of a young woman who came to me for treatment while in the grip of an unhappy love affair. The young woman revealed soon enough that the current affair was not her first disastrous experience with men. She had in fact previously married and divorced a man of lamentably weak character whom she had led around by the nose. He had finally become an habitual alcoholic, and eventually her contempt for him grew to such proportions that they had parted for good.

Fate would seem to have dealt very unkindly with this young woman. From the bare recital of her story, one might conclude that she had ample justification for being suspicious of love and marriage. There were apparently good grounds, at least, for her embittered attitude toward men.

Yet, as we probed into her early background, an entirely new light was cast upon her series of unfortunate experiences. The young woman came of a good family, with a brilliant father who was outstanding in his field. Unhappily, the father was also an arrogant man and something of a bully. He adopted an extremely critical attitude toward his daughter and would constantly censure her behavior, her school work, her clothes, her make-up. He repeatedly questioned her choice of friends and companions. Where she yearned for love and approval, she drew from him only an interminable indictment of everything she did.

Over the years, she developed the only defense available to her—she grew silent and aloof. She learned to conduct herself rigidly, so that her manner became almost masculine. She spoke with sharp and clipped accents in a voice that snapped like a whip. The resentment against her father smoldered constantly and as she grew older it turned into a general hostility toward men.

Unconsciously, the path of love for this young woman became inextricably bound up with the path of aggression. As soon as she was old enough, she left home to get away from her intolerable environment. But when the time came to select a mate of her own, she could not conceive of a substitute love choice without dragging along the dreary baggage of her resentments. She was compelled by her deep early emotional confusion to select a man upon whom she could visit all the antagonism and contempt stored up within her. Her choice of a husband was not an accident of fate. His weak character and ultimate addiction to alcohol provided the perfect pretext for her hostile attitude. Where she once had to submit to the arrogant criticism of her father, she could now take revenge by dominating her husband and treating him with derision.

No one's life can be maintained on a stable basis when the forces of love and hate are thrown so badly out of balance. The young woman's marriage eventually became so painful to her that she had to leave her husband, just as earlier she had been compelled to turn from her father. She had then gone on to a repetition of the old pattern, this time in the form of an unhappy love affair. When that, too, showed signs of breaking up, she developed the symptoms of depression which finally brought her to me for treatment.

It required patient, self-searching effort before this young woman was able to identify the central thread of error in her life. She insisted at first that the unhappiness of her marital and love relationships was entirely due to the character of the men with whom she had been involved. When she finally disentangled her confused paths of emotion, she was able to recognize that she had not only deliberately chosen these men, but by her own behavior had even accentuated their weakest qualities in order to justify her turning upon them with hate.

Love or Perish

In recapitulating her actions, she discovered other erroneous concepts which commonly beguile people into unhappy marriages. She realized that marriage cures nothing —and least of all does it solve anyone's emotional problems. Like many young people who are not at peace with their parents, she had thought that leaving home and finding a husband would lift her emotional distress. When her marriage failed, she had expected that divorce would remedy the situation by enabling her to find a more suitable mate.

In both instances she discovered that the change had altered nothing. Since her own emotional patterns had not changed, the ultimate result was the same. She had merely been caught in the trap of those who think, in the words of Robert Louis Stevenson, that marriage "will sober and change them. Like those who join a brotherhood, they fancy it needs but an act to be out of the coil and clamor forever. But this is a wile of the devil's. To the end, spring winds will sow disquietude, passing faces leave a regret behind them, and the whole world keep calling and calling in their ears. For marriage is like life in this—that it is a field of battle, and not a bed of roses."

When the young woman succeeded at last in relinquishing her false patterns of emotion, she was able to drop the hostile attitude with which she had previously regarded all men. She found, almost as a revelation, that it was then no longer necessary to become involved with weaklings. In the end, she was able to marry a man of character whom she could admire and respect. He was a successful businessman, in his late thirties, whose first wife had died several years before. His business interests happened to be in the textile field, and it turned out that the young woman had a natural talent in matters of design and merchandising. Her husband came to rely more and more on her judgment, and their whole relationship grew into one of mutual love and co-operation.

To Give Is to Gain

A certain amount of self-love is a normal characteristic of every healthy person. To have a proper regard for oneself is indispensable for all work and achievement. If we are too harsh and self-critical of our conduct, our sense of guilt may weaken the will to live and, in extreme cases, bring on actual self-destruction.

With many persons, however, normal self-regard is exaggerated and turned into a morbid fear of giving love freely to others. Originally, the fear is based on a perfectly normal mechanism of our psychic life. The energy of love in its primitive form, as we have seen, is first directed toward one's own body. This primitive path is a biological necessity, since it serves the cause of self-preservation. If we gradually learn to turn some of our self-love to others, it is because the sacrifice leads to an ultimate gain.

But the primitive path is never forgotten. Some of our love energy must at all times remain focused on ourselves. In moments of extreme peril, or on those occasions when we are seriously ill, one can easily observe how all of our energy and interest is withdrawn from others and devoted exclusively to ourselves.

It is the peculiar fate of love, especially in its more passionate form, that it should arouse the ancient danger signals of the primitive psyche. Love, in its intense manifestation between the sexes, is almost literally an abandonment of self. The lover becomes preoccupied exclusively with his beloved and pours forth all his emotional energy in an ecstasy of self-negation. He loses his own individuality, abases himself abjectly, gives up everything he formerly held so precious to himself. For the sake of the beloved, he is even ready to sacrifice his own life.

Wonderful as the experience may be, it cannot persist without becoming a threat to one's self-survival. In such a state, the danger of self-annihilation is very real, for the individual has rendered himself psychically defenseless against outward attack. The normal person inevitably retreats from so extreme a position. To a greater or lesser degree, he must recoil from the beloved in order to restore his own identity.

The flux of love—the oscillation between attraction and repulsion—*is a normal part of every marriage.* True love between two people does not mean that one must become completely absorbed in the other. The partial maintenance of one's own identity is a basic requirement of normal existence, and it would be a fallacy to interpret it as a sign that love has died. When people view marriage in this guise, they may drive themselves to unwarranted accusations, disruptive recriminations, and harmful desires for revenge.

The wise husband and wife know that even the deepest

love must have its intervals of nonactive expression. They do not fall into a panic because they are not the object of each other's ceaseless preoccupation. On the contrary, they realize that a person who makes constant demands for "proofs" of love is like an insecure child who clamors endlessly for his mother's attention. Those who are confident of their basic love will see to it, instead, that provision is made for release of the tensions and hostilities inevitable in every intimate association. Each will make sure that the other is allowed his own measure of independent thought and activity, with periods when the accumulated aggressions may be worked off in sports, hobbies or other channels of deflection.

It is another matter entirely when the normal need for self-assertion is turned into a morbid form in which the flow of love becomes permanently fixed on one's own self. Such people are unable to choose a love partner on the basis of a realistic evaluation. They can love only those who are reflections of themselves and who demand no reciprocal adjustment to their own personalities. They invariably over-idealize their chosen objects of love, and will endow them with imaginary qualities built solely on the fantasy pattern of their own image.

When the period of disillusion inevitably arrives, such persons cast aside their love choices in utter repudiation. For them, the mutual compromises and sacrifices of normal love are an impossible barrier to hurdle. Since they love only their own image, they cannot even bear to recognize the needs of anyone not completely devoted to their own interests. They can only go on to new objects of love with whom they can repeat the path of overidealization, disillusion and repudiation. Each time, like so many Hollywood actresses, they proclaim loudly to all the world that they have at last found the "one, perfect love." Three months later, they emerge hopefully from the divorce court, often on the arm of a new, "perfect" love.

To be thus caught on the treadmill of one's own personality is to be chained to an infantile fear of being "swallowed up" by the dominating mother. The victims of this fear usually show a history of intense attachment to a mother who, in turn, placed undue stress upon her own attachment to her child. In an emotional constellation of this kind, where overemphasis is the basic pattern, the demands upon the child become intolerably oppressive. He finds insupportable the price he must pay for love, and in self-defense turns away from the mother with a permanent fear of all entanglements.

This fear may also arise because of one's infantile disappointment in the mother. Every child is insatiable in its demands for love. Some mothers either do not give enough love, or they handle the ceaseless demands with unnecessary harshness. The child then withdraws its tendrils of love in bitterness. Like a ship that has missed its moorings, it floats off on a sea of emotional loneliness and never again will attempt an anchorage.

Out of this disappointment is born the dream of a perfect love that will impose no burdens and require no sacrifices. Yet it must be understood once and for all that the paradise of perfect love has never been on sea or land, nor can it ever come to pass. The blissful aspiration of complete pleasure and no pain, of instant satisfaction and no denial, of constant peace and no tension—this is a childish illusion that violates the truths of human life and is doomed to inexorable disappointment.

The basic biological facts of life show how impossible is this aspiration. We would never eat if chemical changes in the body did not produce the discomforts and pangs of hunger. We would never breathe if changes in the blood did not produce the suffocating carbon dioxide that stimulates the reflexes of breathing.

So in our psychic life, it is the creation and then the relaxation of tension that drive the living organism forward to activity. From the very first breath of life, the human psyche must learn to counter aggression with love. We must learn to tolerate pain, to brook delay, to compromise with the environment. We must learn to accomodate ourselves to the world outside if we would win love and protection. We must accept the truth that in mature life one must give in order to gain. The paradise of perfect love is only in the womb, and he who seeks to recapture that bliss does so at the peril of losing life itself. "Comfort's in heaven," wrote Shakespeare, "and we are on earth."

The Dream of Heavenly Love

There is another dream of ideal love, deeply embedded in modern Western culture, which creates great emotional havoc in the lives of many men. It is the dream of a pure love, spiritually exalted, in which sensual desire has no part. Celebrated by poets and philosophers alike, it opposes "heavenly" and "earthly" love as the twin poles of man's nature, and it implies a measure of nobility for those who can attain the higher level transcending base animal appetite.

As an ethical concept embodying the ideal of a sublime good, the dream has undoubtedly spurred men on to notable deeds in the annals of civilization. It has played an important role in many of the world's great religions, serving as a basic tenet of faith that has helped curb the more destructive aspects of our primitive nature. Artists have for many centuries found it a fertile source of inspiration; they have enshrined its spirit of aspiration in the devout scenes of early Christian painting, the soaring lines of medieval cathedrals, and the majestic melodies of Renaissance music. In literature, too, it has been a major theme for treatment by great writers from Dante and Malory down to Tennyson and Thomas Hardy.

Unfortunately, the dream also betrays a profound psychic cleavage that may lead, in everyday life, to tragic emotional disruption. The attempt to separate the sensual currents of love from the tender or ideal aspects in marriage is at bottom an infantile illusion which cannot be maintained in adult life without serious damage to one's happiness and stability. If carried out in one's actual emotional behavior, it makes normal love in marriage between men and women an utter impossibility. Especially in men, it is the cause of a certain kind of psychic impotency which is responsible for widespread disturbances in married life.

Paths to Successful Marriage

From my experience, I believe at least one-fourth of all divorces stem from this source.

From a realistic standpoint, the inability to fuse the tender with the sensual streams of love leads men to divide women into two general classes. On the one hand are the "good" women whom they can admire and respect, but toward whom they cannot direct the full force of their passion. On the other hand are the "low" or inferior women who may be used to satisfy their sexual desires, but who can never merit genuine respect or be considered as potential wives and mothers. Men who hold these views of women oscillate between the two types in a permanent state of confusion and anxiety. They derive full happiness from neither, and are rent by a constant sense of guilt toward both.

In severe cases, such men are incapable of marriage altogether. They are like the composer Brahms, who all his life fell in love secretly with women of quality, but could never express his passion to any except professional prostitutes. Other men so biased are driven by the nature of their sensual requirements to marry women far beneath them in social or intellectual status. We then have such tragic spectacles as the great poet Heine wed to a woman of the streets whose shrewish tongue humiliated him constantly in public, and whose lack of comprehension led her to use his manuscripts as wrapping paper for dirty laundry.

The more common way in which such men resolve the problem is to marry a woman of equal status, but to seek outlets from women of a lower class for the sensual side of their natures. Their lives then usually follow a pattern

81

of increasing strife and dissatisfaction in marriage. Their wives in turn find the expected happiness of wedded life to be a bitter mirage, and the situation often degenerates into open warfare. Ultimately, such men either succumb to serious illness or are driven to wreck their home life beyond repair.

The typical path they follow is illustrated by the case of an advertising executive whose wife once consulted me in her despair. Her husband was a man of considerable achievement in his profession and had risen to a post that carried a salary of $75,000 a year. After the first bloom had passed from their marriage, he began to spend more and more of his time away from home. Three daughters were born of the marriage, and as they grew up he became increasingly irritable and hostile in his behavior. He began to drink heavily and to be promiscuous in his relations with women. By the time the daughters reached their teens, his conduct was completely insupportable. He got to hating both wife and children, and would openly curse "those damned women" around the house.

One week end he went off on a fishing trip with a party of men that included the head of his firm and some very important clients. That Saturday night in camp he got terribly drunk, and in a mood of perverse rebellion assailed his boss with a stream of filthy, abusive language. Next day he was subdued and contrite—but the damage had been done. When he arrived at his desk on the Monday morning, he found a message from his boss stating that he was summarily fired and had ten minutes to get his belongings out of the office.

The executive obtained another post, but this time the

salary was only $10,000 a year. His drinking increased, and his behavior at home became ever more scandalous. The effect upon the children was so bad that his wife finally could tolerate it no longer. Failing in all efforts to effect an improvement, she obtained a divorce and took the children away with her.

Her husband—now alone and without even the semblance of external restraint—sank rapidly in his professional life. He lost one job after another, until the field became virtually closed to him. In the end he drifted off to another city, where he ultimately became a day laborer.

Although the path of collapse in marriage is not always so dramatically sharp, the essential features remain the same whenever there is this fatal division in the husband's emotional life. Such men are unable to accept their wives fully as both spiritual and sexual partners, and as a consequence neither true companionship nor true love ever develops between them. A sense of duty may for a time preserve the outward forms of the marriage, but underneath this pretense a mounting current of disappointment and hostility keeps fraying the edges of the marital bond. More and more the husband will tend to seek his satisfactions away from home, either with a mistress or in a series of turbulent affairs. As an alternative, he may become an alcoholic or lapse into wholly irresponsible behavior.

The wife, on her part, may seek to compensate for her own frustration by turning her love in an exaggerated and unhealthy form upon her children. It is a substitute device responsible for the phenomenon so often noted in American life, where the activities of wife and children dominate the home and the husband appears only as an incidental appendage to the family unit. But this, too, is likely to prove unavailing in the final analysis, and the picture will at last be so barren as to destroy all possibilities of a happy marriage.

Men so afflicted are invariably those whose emotional patterns are rooted in the path of childhood. Their fundamental disturbance arises from the morbid separation of love's energy into two hostile currents that remain at war with each other whenever an attempt at adult love is set in motion. They are bound to their earlier attitudes toward their mothers, when erotic expressions of love were forbidden to accompany the tender manifestations. All of us were subjected to this repression in the usual course of childhood, but normally men outgrow such early proscriptions. They are able to fuse the tender and sensual currents once more, and to direct the united stream toward mature substitute love objects without guilt.

When men refuse to adopt the mature course, it is because the earlier proscription has been fixed as a permanent impediment to the full expression of love. Against this background, they are unconsciously unable to view a "good" woman as anything but a re-creation of the mother in her original form. The childhood barriers against erotic expression are then revived, and in inward fright they recoil from the full consummation of their love. The inhibition is especially accentuated after the arrival of children, when the young wife more and more appears in realistic guise as an actual mother.

Men and women burdened by this widely prevalent pattern of love and marriage need guidance so that they can realize where the true basis of their difficulties lies. It is futile to expect that moral condemnation, on the one hand, or appeals to reason, on the other, will remedy a situation so complex and so deeply bound up with childhood patterns. Nor should they deceive themselves with the thought that erroneous choice of each other may have been responsible in the first place for their problem. Only an actual release of the early barriers to love can effect a permanent solution. Often, the best psychiatric help is necessary.

It is especially important that young men and women do not allow themselves to be caught in this harrowing pattern. The idealistic concept of love is a normal phase of adolescence which has a definite value. By creating a partial inhibition of the erotic impulse, it serves a useful purpose in civilization, for it leads to the development of those tender strains of love, freed from sensual impulses, so necessary for permanent and stable relationships in society.

What young people must guard against is the extreme inhibition which dissociates the two strains of love altogether. Frequently I am consulted by young wives who reveal that even after a year or more of marriage their husbands have been unwilling to participate in sexual relations. The avowed basis of refusal usually is a belief that sexual relations would be "justified" only when they had decided to have children.

Actually, the rejection turns out to be the result either of a deep psychic inhibition or a false concept of the role sexuality plays in life. Human beings are sexual beings, and it is now a generally accepted fact that sex is a normal and necessary part of our lives. As Dean Pike, of the Cathedral of St. John the Divine, has said, "Sex has a threefold purpose. It is a sacrament of unity; it is for enjoyment; and it is for procreation." The denial of this fundamental truth is always an ominous sign. It presages lifelong unhappiness and should be subjected to correction at the earliest possible moment if a stable and enduring marriage is to be expected.

Men follow a futile goal when they seek to attain sublimity in love through a total denial of its basic source. Our true aspiration must be rather to achieve control of our primitive nature so that we may employ our normal energies in the best service of mankind. To attempt the abandonment of that primitive heritage is more than impossible: it can only release the very demons we hope to exorcise.

A Formula for Happy Marriage

True love between a man and a woman may be defined as a relationship in which each helps to preserve and enlarge the life of the other. Such a love presupposes in both a maturity of emotional expression, free of childish compulsions to exploit, to dominate or to destroy. It is based on an acceptance of one another's specific biological nature, with the recognition that man and woman are complementary, not hostile, to each other. It knows that each can fulfill his own destiny only by collaborative effort with the other in carrying out life's immemorial design. Mature love thrives therefore on a realistic basis of equal exchange which sets up a benign circle of mutual pleasure, reassurance and inspiration. It is the mechanism that creates a permanently stable balance in the lifelong struggle with the disruptive forces of aggression.

Marriage, to be successful, must be founded on a relationship of this kind. Only then may we expect it to be proof against the world's uncertainties and stresses. Only when so constituted will marriage free the wellspring of love to flow in accord with joint needs as well as individual desires. It will then serve not as a rigid harness that shackles life and stifles development, but as a pliant instrument that facilitates constant growth and expansion. It will give staunch support when this is imperative, yield freedom and independence when these are desirable, maintain caution or abandon as the true need dictates.

For true marriage, while it is a vehicle of love, is also a framework for life itself. It cannot be confined to the narrow ledge of petty pleasure or personal safety. To endure, it must also be an avenue into the world outside, serving as a source of nourishment and inspiration for the many tasks of society as a whole.

A marriage based on mature love will have this boldness of outlook and adventurousness of spirit. It will brush aside the distracting claims of personal vanities and momentary fears. It will be a joint undertaking in which the man and woman will dedicate their hearts to mutual uplifting and the strengthening of life as a whole. It will be the kind of union that Goethe had in view when he wrote: "The sum which two married people owe to one another defies calculation. It is an infinite debt, which can only be discharged through all eternity."

CHAPTER FIVE

Love's Cradle

A NEWBORN infant is in many ways a rather curious bundle of paradox. Tiny, undeveloped and ignorant of the world it has just entered, it nevertheless brings with it a biological structure perfected by millions of years of evolution, with the wisdom of the ages in each of its cells. Physically it is so feeble that it cannot protect itself against the smallest enemy; yet the instinctual drives it inherits are as powerful as those of any jungle animal. Even in appearance the baby offers a striking contrast. Though poised on the threshold of life, it turns to us a wrinkled, frowning little face that might almost be the wizened countenance of an ancient and world-weary patriarch.

Like other living organisms, the infant in time outgrows most of the incongruities present at birth. Yet one basic paradox remains to plague its entire course of growth and development. Whereas plants and animals flourish by spontaneously obeying their instinctual drives, the human being can survive in harmony with his environment only if he learns to *curb* his primitive impulses. In this respect he is unique among nature's children. Other organisms may be required to adapt themselves to external conditions; but their vital life processes continue to function freely, without internal interference. Man alone among earth's creatures is burdened with the task of inhibiting and modifying his own fundamental drives.

The burden is invoked at birth and weighs heavily upon man for the rest of his days. Right at the beginning, the infant is compelled to regulate its hunger instinct according to artificial restrictions found nowhere else in nature. Soon afterward the child must learn to control his bodily evacuations in conformity with rules imposed by the will of others. His instinctual expressions of aggression are meanwhile opposed from the start; and as the child grows older these are curbed with increasing severity in proportion to their strength. On top of this, the normal sexual instinct is subjected to a multitude of taboos that restrict its free expression from childhood all through maturity.

Mankind has been willing to accept restrictions upon its primitive drives because in exchange it has won greater security of life. But the child knows nothing of this ultimate gain. It lives only for the immediate moment, and cannot be expected to balance future rewards against present sacrifices. It can undergo frustration and self-denial only as painful experiences that do violence to its deepest needs.

There is another obligation, besides, that is vastly more urgent and compelling for the child. *It must grow!* As an undeveloped organism, its fundamental objective must be to negotiate the arduous and lengthy path of development that stretches ahead to maturity. Nature imperiously spurs the child on to concentrate upon this cardinal goal. Society may be properly concerned with training the child's primitive drives to conform with acceptable patterns of behavior. But the child itself must use its instinctual energies to build bone and muscle, to expand its personality, to hew a place for itself in a strange and stubborn world. *The child must first live before it can conform.*

Every conscientious parent is thus faced with a dual task that might well challenge the wisdom of a Solomon. He is called upon to gratify the child's instinctual demands, on the one hand, and to deny them on the other. He must protect the child at every turn because of its weak and helpless position—yet he knows that it will not be able to function resolutely in life unless it is also allowed to meet and overcome dangers on its own. If the parent follows one vaunted aim of education, he will encourage the child to reach toward independence of thought and action. If he obeys another and equally powerful claim, he will insist that the child comply with fixed social ideals. The parent, in brief, must both chain and liberate the child at one and the same time.

As if this were not sufficiently formidable an undertaking, the parent is asked to work a further miracle! He is asked to transform the primitive and even savage child into a tolerant, co-operative and loving human adult.

For the lesson of love must be learned in the cradle if it is to be learned at all. It is here that the infant is first taught its patterns of reaction to the outside world. Only here, as the pupil of its mother, can the child learn how to give and receive love. It is the skill of the parental hand, shaping the child's course during the formative years, which largely determines how well he will resolve the inevitable conflicts with his environment. Fate leaves parents no choice but to be the main channel through which every child either inherits mankind's best wisdom or falls victim to its grossest crimes and stupidities.

If parents falter in carrying out so monumental a responsibility, who will dare apportion blame? Human nature is a wild labyrinth of mysterious forces for which none of us has the master chart. Even so wise a scientist as Dr. A. A. Brill, America's pioneer psychoanalyst, observed near the close of his long career that "we have just scratched the surface of the human soul." Since each infant confronts us anew with the ancient maze, one need not wonder that parents stumble in the effort to penetrate its secret passageways. The marvel is rather that they achieve any measure of success at all.

Muscle Tensions

Though much of the human labyrinth still remains an enigma, modern psychology has already explored some of its main corridors. Especially significant are the discoveries made in our study of early childhood. Here we have obtained profound insights that can help parents solve some of

Love or Perish

the fundamental problems likely to arise during this crucial period.

One of the basic concepts every parent should grasp is that a child begins to form its character and personality as soon as it enters the world. The human infant is not a simple, unknowing creature whose needs are fully satisfied merely by food and warmth. Observation shows, instead, that it is an extraordinarily wise and complex organism, charged with imperious instinctual desires. When these primitive needs come into conflict with the external environment, embodied in the person of the mother or nurse, there is at once set off a chain of profound emotional reactions. The infant is acutely sensitive to the attitudes and behavior of those upon whose care its life depends, and it begins to build its characteristic patterns of love and hate the moment it is first touched after birth.

Adults have in the past been misled into assuming that the child, because it lacks the power of speech, also lacks powers of perception. The truth is that the human infant, like any primitive animal, is marvelously aware of everything that affects its welfare. It has the capacity to read what one may call our "muscle tensions"—those silent, but eloquent, betrayers of our true emotional attitudes.

In civilized life, we ordinarily must exert self-control over our emotions—whether of love, or hate, or fear. But an emotion automatically tends to be expressed in action. No matter how great our self-restraint, we usually indicate our inner feelings by some kind of muscular movement, however faint or involuntary. We show our emotions by a movement of the eye, by the set of the muscles in our face, by the pitch, volume and rhythm of the voice. We convey our feelings unwittingly, too, by the way we stand or walk, by the touch of our hand, and by such things as the dampness or dryness of the skin. That is how animals understand us so well, even when we do not say a word.

It is through these muscle tensions that the mother transmits her true feelings to her child. And it is through her manner and attitude while caring for it that the child learns to develop security or fear. To the adult, feeding and dressing a baby may appear as routine duties without special significance. But to the infant, these apparently innocuous events are momentous adventures which enable it to discover the nature and meaning of the outside world. They represent the impact of environment, affording the child its first experiences of pleasure and pain, of gratification and frustration, of love and hate, security and fear.

The newborn infant is by itself unprepared to evaluate these terrifying experiences. It is torn between its own selfish instinctual impulses and the outward demands that are suddenly imposed without warning. The mother is the only one who can guide the harassed little creature through the seething emotional whirlpool. *Her love is the child's only possible reward for the painful sacrifices and adjustments it is called upon to make.* The infant registers her approval or disapproval as a seismograph catches the faintest tremor of the earth. The mother's confidence becomes the child's confidence; her antagonism, a shattering catastrophe.

Psychiatric research has shown that the child's success or failure in negotiating these hazardous first steps depends largely on the parent's emotional attitudes. An anxious young mother, for example, may try her best to conceal her agitated feelings, but through her muscle tensions the infant will perceive the true state of affairs infallibly. It may react by nursing badly, and indigestion will follow. If the mother's disturbed condition persists, the child may form symptoms of serious illness. I have seen infants who, at the age of only two months, had already developed real neuroses because of the way they had been handled by their mothers and fathers. The infants had absorbed the parents' anxieties like a blotter.

Not all children, it is true, react alike to the same conditions. Human beings differ in their inherited nervous constitutions, much as animals do. The Great Dane, for instance, is a quiet, dignified and somewhat slow-moving dog, while the terrier is a nervous and active animal, responding quickly to stimuli. Things that upset a terrier may pass virtually unnoticed by the Great Dane. Children similarly vary in their nervous susceptibilities. Some, for example, are especially sensitive to sound, and their reactions may be as extreme as those of the great composer, Mozart, who as a little boy fainted away the first time he heard the peal of a trumpet. Others remain undisturbed by loud noises, and even delight in them.

Yet these constitutional differences, while they may affect intensity of development, do not alter the basic mechanisms by which character and personality are formed. Given the original heritage, what happens subsequently to the child's character is in every case largely determined by the emotional background against which he first moved on the stage of life.

The parent remains the great prompter who teaches the infant actor the main lines, gestures and inflections of his future role. If the parent's demeanor in the prompter's box is one of steadfastness and love, the child will be encouraged to use his strength with skill and control. He will be prevailed upon to abandon willful impediments that serve to hamper his art. He will learn to retain personal idiosyncrasies when these lend grace and enchantment to his performance. Yet he will sacrifice them willingly if it means adding beauty and power to the total stage effect.

But if the parent is an overbearing tyrant, or is confused in his directions, he will train a player forever unsure of his basic cues. The little novice will move with intimidated step and speak with strangulated voice, always fearful of his audience. He will not dare to construct his own interpretations, and will be able to learn the lessons of life only by rote. At times he will become filled with secret rebellion; but then he will be able to assert his identity only through vain mannerisms or grotesque actions that will serve as a dragging weight upon the rest of the ensemble. Unable to believe in the strength of his own excellence, he will seek to attract attention to himself by paltry little devices: he will jockey for the spotlight, steal scenes, quarrel with his fellow players. If none of these avail, he may flee the stage at a crisis and thus ruin the performance altogether.

A wise parent, like a wise director, will therefore seek to avoid extremes in the handling of his charges. He will neither overindulge the child's whims, nor will he insist on imposing his own rigid interpretations. This point is well stated in the recent symposium, *The Church and Mental Health,* where Dr. Gotthard Booth writes: "Love means that the adult be genuinely concerned with the evolution of the true nature of the child. Children are not able to respond to a love which tries to fashion them according to the concept of an adult, no matter how good the latter's intentions may be." The parents' goal, that is, must be to let the child discover its own nature and capacities, and then lead it to use those capacities in their most effective relationship with the outside world.

Such a parent will balance restraint with freedom, compulsion with inspiration, restriction with adventure. He will know that *a wise love is that which is designed mainly to support the child while it learns to adjust to the demands of the world.* A child who grows up inwardly confident that he has had this kind of love from his parents is armed with the most powerful weapon on earth. Children so equipped possess the calm, deep courage that makes heroes and heroines in real life.

The Magic Reward

"Give a little love to a child, and you get a great deal back," wrote John Ruskin, hitting shrewdly upon the secret of all child education. Civilization, too, has long known that love is the magic reward for which man is willing to yield some part of his savagery. Still, neither Ruskin nor the wisest of the prophets has ever been able to determine the precise "little" or "great deal" of love that each child needs for its own best welfare.

Yet this is the crux of the problem that faces all conscientious parents. At what point of the child's scale will they find the "adequate" mark on which to balance their love? If they are too harsh in their demands upon the child and do not give him enough love, he will be crippled in his ability to cope with his environment. He may become sullen and backward, or rebellious and overaggressive. In either case he will feel rejected and robbed of his due, thus creating a permanent distortion of his personality and his faith in love.

Equally harmful effects will follow if the parents lavish too much love upon the child. He may become too strongly dependent in his emotional life, requiring a constant support and protection that will weaken his capacity to face stern realities alone. He may grow to feel dominated by his parents' love, and to resent the price he is compelled to pay in return. In that case he will learn to fear love as a burden, and to hate all those who make its claims upon him.

The children who suffer from inadequate parental love are not merely those who are the victims of outright brutality or neglect. They may appear in any family, and they form a representative part of every group. I had an unusual opportunity to study one such "average" child when she was a little girl of four in nursery school, and then to follow up her life until she was thirty. The little girl came from a well-to-do family and had originally been its center of attention. But when a brother was born, the emphasis of love was shifted to the little newcomer.

The two children attended the nursery school together, and the mother used to call for them at the end of the day. She was always kind and friendly in her attitude toward her daughter, but her face would visibly light up with joy as she greeted the little boy. The father, too, was so delighted with the birth of a son and heir that his attentions to the little girl dwindled noticeably.

I remember being in a neighborhood store with a friend one day, when the mother came in with the two children to do some shopping. The little girl tagged after her mother and brother in a forlorn way, and all the time she kept pleading in a plaintive and pitiful voice: "I want a five-cent bar of Ivory soap . . . I want a five-cent bar of Ivory soap!"

When they had left, my friend turned to me with anguish and distress written across his face. "I feel as though something dreadful had just happened," he said. "That child's voice—I've never been so upset and depressed by a thing like that!"

And, indeed, the child's apparently senseless request seemed altogether inadequate a cause in itself for my friend's profound reaction. It was only because of my familiarity with the family background that I was able to interpret the incident for him. The child's forlorn little plea was in truth a tragic appeal. She was the rejected member of the family, filled with loneliness and anxiety, and the words of her mournful plaint might just as well have been: "Won't you love me, please? . . . Won't you love me?"

Love's Cradle

In the nursery school the little girl proved quite a problem. She went around constantly appealing to the teachers for love: she wanted to touch them and to be petted by them in return. She did not get along well with the other children. But she was a bright youngster and went through school and college with a good record, though at no time did she make many friends.

At the age of 24 she married a man who turned out to be an alcoholic. They had a child; but the husband's drunken sprees and frequent absences from home soon created a situation so bad that a divorce followed. A few years later the girl was married again, this time to a man whose background was completely alien to her own. It turned out that he had been interested only in her money. He behaved with such outrageous promiscuity that this union also ended in a divorce.

The picture here is clearly one of a little girl who had all the outward care a child might need. Yet the early background showed a pattern of emotional rejection by both mother and father. Like all childhood patterns, this one became engraved upon her unconscious memory as a model for compulsive repetition in the future. She was literally bound by the memory, and therefore had a strong drive to repeat in adult form the rejection that had been hers as a child.

A faulty emotional background of an opposite, but equally "average" type was illustrated in the case of a young man who came to me because of professional difficulties. An assistant master at a famous boys' school, he had been twice passed over in favor of new staff members when a promotion was due. He was naturally upset and depressed by his failure to advance.

It turned out that he was a kind and gentle man, well liked by the boys at the school, but a somewhat deprecatory and passive person obviously lacking in force and leadership. He had been one of two children, born ten years after his brother, during a period when his father was away in the army in the First World War. The father returned partly disabled, and the mother was compelled to go out into the business world and help support the family.

The mother became quite successful; but she was a very domineering woman. Though she loved the little boy, she made it quite clear by her unconscious attitudes that he would lose her love if he did not behave exactly as she wanted him to.

Another child, with a different kind of nervous system, might have become rebellious and refused to submit. But this boy had a gentle nature and could not resist his mother's control. "She used to cut me down with quiet, ironic sarcasm whenever I expressed thoughts or wishes that she disagreed with," he told me. "That frightened me more than physical punishment ever would have done."

The fear of asserting himself and of expressing his views carried over into maturity. Although he was a bright young man, the lifelong domination by his mother's image prevented him from becoming a vigorous and normally combative individual. We were able to overcome some of his passivity, and in time he won his promotion.

Between the extremes illustrated by these two cases lies a balanced middle ground where the magic reward of love is neither withheld nor used as a means of intimidation. To estimate when and to what degree it should be dispensed is a delicate and difficult task. Parents have asked me innumerable times just how this can be determined; but there is no single rule to follow. The ultimate decision will vary with different children, and at different times with the same child. The only accurate guide is the individual child himself. If he is too passive and docile in his acceptance of things, or if his aggression is so great that he constantly comes into conflict with the people around him, then the child's needs are not being properly met, and the parent will know that the balance of love is askew.

To remedy these situations, the parents' own attitudes sometimes require correction. In striving to do what is best for their children, for example, many parents neglect to do what is best for themselves. They may send their children to expensive schools even though they cannot afford it, or they may stint on their own wardrobes in order to have the children fashionably dressed. Here, the unconscious motive often is not to help the child, but to make up for real or imaginary deprivations that the parents themselves may have suffered in their own childhood. But this almost never works out properly. It does not give the children what they themselves need, and hence the parents are often left bewildered because their well-meaning efforts result in no real benefit to anyone.

Parents must also realize that their love for their children cannot always take the same form of expression. The newborn infant requires a maximum of protective love that flows fully and freely in its most elemental form. But this kind of love will smother a child if it is maintained too far beyond the infantile period. As the child's ego grows in strength, the parent's love will show itself in respectful consideration of the child's new individuality. He will then express love in the form of quiet approval or disapproval, using this means as an incentive to win the child's co-operation in curbing its own excesses of behavior. Still later, when the child's conscience has developed fully, the thoughtful parent will take an opposite tack. He will express his love by an easy and relaxed attitude, for at this period a child often suffers by being too severe with himself and may need help in moderating his own harsh sense of morality.

A parent will automatically adopt the appropriate attitude if his constant objective is to encourage the child to grow. Parents who forget this primary goal often find it difficult to keep pace with the rapid succession of stages through which every child passes, and they tend to resist each new development. They need to be reminded that the best tribute to their success as parents will be the speed with which the child reaches the point where they are no longer needed.

Teacher—or Policeman?

Every child compels its parents to go through the whole history of civilization all over again. Just as the human embryo recapitulates the story of evolution, so the child

Love's Cradle

repeats in rapid succession the many stages of development that carried men from primitive savagery to contemporary culture. The parent must accompany the child on this difficult journey, acting as chief interpreter and guide. He must give the directions at each turn of the trail, and it will be largely due to his skill if the child emerges finally as a loving and balanced human being.

If many parents, despite their best efforts, fail to achieve this ultimate goal with their children, it is usually because they misconceive a central aspect of their role. Most of us understand fully the part we must play as good providers for our children. We readily comprehend the measures that must be taken to protect them from danger, to fill their nutritional needs, and to assure their physical health and development as they move along the path to maturity.

What throws most parents into confusion and bewilderment is the basic problem of curbing the child's primitive impulses. Each new member of the human race brings with him all the ancient threats and fears that mankind has struggled so long to subdue. In every child's unconscious mind lie the crawling beasts of selfish aggression, of murderous hate, and of powerful sexual drives that will run rampant if not controlled.

The parent is the delegate appointed by civilization to tame these destructive forces. It is a mighty responsibility —yet most of us are given precious little equipment with which to carry it out! Our instruction book usually contains little but our past fears and our own faltering solutions as the models to follow. If we look at human history for our cue, we see that the emphasis has almost invariably been focused on the technique of suppression rather than of enlightened guidance. Mankind, faced with its own stubbornness and recalcitrance, has always found it easier to take the role of a stern policeman than of a loving teacher.

Few intelligent persons today accept the code of condign punishment to the degree once traditional in child education. Yet many parents still remain baffled by the challenge to which they are put. Children today, as always, obviously cannot be brought up without discipline. They are little savages, and must be taught to accept the many frustrations that life itself makes inevitable. Most parents see no alternative but to adopt a stringent severity in their moral attitude toward their children, even while conceding that the lash may no longer be considered the most effective instrument for inculcating discipline.

The answer to this viewpoint is simple. Suppression does not work! We need only glance around at our neighbors to see the toll it exacts in unhappiness, sickness and morbidly twisted personalities. The technique of suppression merely perpetuates the evils it hopes to abolish. It does not eliminate or even hold back the destructive drives in human nature—it merely forces them into hidden recesses where, like steam under pressure, they must eventually explode.

Parents are led into this falsely harsh attitude toward their children largely because of unconscious processes *in themselves*. Their agitation over the child's destructive impulses is based not simply on concern for the child's best welfare. It also springs from the fact that the child's behavior revives the parent's own buried primitive impulses and unconsciously recalls his own fearful struggles to bring them under control. *The parent becomes frightened as much by his own secret residue of primitive desires as he is by the child's open expression of them.*

It is this unconscious reaction which often prevents parents from handling the child's behavior problems on a reality basis. Because the parent's own forbidden impulses are involved, he grows overintense in his emotional attitudes, magnifies the significance of the child's offense, and takes restrictive measures far out of proportion to the actual need. *It is as if the parent must get angry enough to punish himself as well as the child.* There is psychological truth in the ancient joke about the irate father, who, whip in hand, interrupts the chastisement of his little boy to say: "Son, this hurts me more than it does you!"

Children are rarely deceived in these matters. Unconsciously they sense the parent's mixed emotions, divining the secret guilt responsible for the undue severity of the punishment. They are thrown into inner confusion by this knowledge. Some children, as a result, are led to question the culpability of their own misdeeds, and what finally remains in their minds is a bitter resentment of injustice rather than an acceptance of the need to control their primitive drives. In later life, they will tend to give free rein to their impulses, however destructive or antisocial these may be. Their main concern will be simply to avoid punishment.

Other children may react to the parent's disproportionate intensity by forming an oversevere conscience of their own. They will develop a pervasive sense of unworthiness, suffering constant guilt for the most trivial offense. Such children will never become loving human beings. They will deem themselves unworthy of love, for one thing. They will also seek to blame other people for many of their own real or imagined defects, and thus will be unable to love others in turn.

The parent who wishes his child to grow up into a normal and balanced adult must therefore free himself of the undue anxieties which are at the bottom of all suppressive measures. He must bear in mind that the child's primitive impulses are the source of his energies throughout life. They must be controlled; but to stifle them will seriously injure the child's normal drive and normal curiosity.

Children express their primitive drives in rawest form not because they are evil, but because they know no other way. To play policeman and punish them as criminals is a profound violation of their nature. *Their behavior would be criminal in an adult, but it is a perfectly normal mode of expression for a child*. Often we need only wait, and the objectionable phases of the behavior pass away of their own accord. At other times, it needs only a touch of kindly guidance to be steered into useful and constructive paths.

All children, for example, pass through a cruel stage. They pull wings off butterflies, torture kittens, or skin frogs. I once had occasion to deal with such a problem when one little girl in nursery school took to biting the other children in her class. Things reached a climax when she left her teeth marks in the cheek of a little boy. We solved the situation by putting the little girl in a play pen on one side of the room. "If you bite other children," the teacher told her, "you can't play with them."

The little girl kicked and screamed in protest during the

Love's Cradle

first day of isolation. On the second day she voluntarily promised not to bite any more children if the teacher would let her rejoin her playmates. She was allowed to do so, and the problem never arose again.

The great trick is always to treat the child's behavior as a normal manifestation, and simply to divert it to better uses whenever the realities of life so dictate. This does not mean that we must dispense with firmness, discipline or even a normal amount of anger toward our children. (If your basic attitude is one of loving kindness, you may yell at children and even cuff them around a bit without doing any real harm.) It means that we will not impose the *needless* frustrations, the *unjustified* punishments, the *projected* guilts that cause so much damage. It means that we will choose the role of the wise teacher who, with love, leads his pupil into love.

CHAPTER SIX

The Glory of the Senses

Nature has endowed every normal person with wonderful equipment for the potential enjoyment of life. Its gift is embodied in the marvelous structure of the human nervous system, whose delicate sensory apparatus gives each of us an infinite capacity to perceive and partake of the endless bounty that the world affords. On a primitive level, our organs of perception are designed to gain knowledge of the external environment for purposes of self-protection. But if his senses are fully attuned to all their tensile vigor, man can be like some magnificent Aeolian harp—free to catch all the jubilant winds of the universe, ready to respond harmoniously with his own melodies of joy and affirmation.

Love itself may be defined as the ability to use our sensory apparatus to its fullest degree. For love, in its widest meaning, is simply *an intense, positive interest in an object.* When we love a thing, we become deeply engrossed in it

The Glory of the Senses

with all our senses. This is true whether the thing we love is a woman or a flower, a food or a landscape, a song or a philosophical theory. In each case we want to come into the closest possible contact with it—to look at it, touch it, listen to it. It is through this kind of union with the beloved object that we are able, by means of our senses, to obtain pleasure and inspiration.

All of our most exalted moments in life bear this imprint of profound absorption and concentration. In the rapture of union between a man and a woman, it is as if our bodies and all our sensations blend completely with the beloved person. A comparable unity invests every great achievement in all phases of life. The inventor in pursuit of a new discovery works at his models with a depth of attention that blots out all else in the world. The sculptor who creates a new form of beauty shapes each curve with an intensity of purpose that is almost fierce in its devotion.

Watch any accomplished artisan at work—a musical virtuoso with his instrument, a master craftsman with his tools—and the most striking feature of the performance is its grave and noble concentration. Behind the great deeds of any leader, whether in religion or science or industry, there is the same story of senses and energies marshaled to their utmost pitch of efficiency. One may even declare it as a law that achievement of any kind is possible only where there is complete attention to the task at hand—which is but another way of saying that we may expect success only if we love what we do.

This does not mean that the gifted few are alone capable of true achievement. The truth is that all of us attain the greatest success and happiness possible in this life whenever we use our native capacities to their fullest extent. There is as much joy for the farmer who toils with utmost skill to reap the maximum harvest from his acre of soil as there is for the engineer who builds an ingenious bridge across the torrents of a raging river. So, too, the husband and wife in any city apartment who give each other a lifetime of true devotion have won a prize of love to match any that Darby and Joan may have achieved.

The obstacle that faces most of us is not lack of special talents. What blocks us from the path of full achievement is rather our failure to use the natural endowment that is every man's birthright. Yet it is one of the tragedies of civilized life that ordinary attempts to overcome this failure bring us inevitably into conflict with prevailing social standards and ideals. Society, with its primary emphasis on order and regulation, demands that to a considerable extent we sacrifice our primitive animal heritage for the sake of communal safety and stability.

Society does this, ironically enough, through education. From earliest childhood we are forbidden by parents, nurses and teachers to give full and uninhibited play to our natural impulses. In one respect, of course, education must inevitably take such a course. Man's natural drives also include dangerous impulses toward murder, incest and cannibalism; and we would long ago have destroyed each other if no restrictions had been imposed. But education, in its effort to control these destructive forces, often makes an unnecessary error. It attempts to throttle our original impulses altogether, where its purpose should rather be to direct them toward constructive channels.

No one, for example, will deny the need to inculcate the principle that we must not attack and kill our fellow men. It is another matter entirely, however, when we punish a little child because his instinctual curiosity has led him to touch and tear a book that has been left on the library table. Again, we cannot allow a little child to wander at will into the parental bedroom at night. Yet this does not mean that we must take harsh measures of reprisal when a child quite naturally tries to examine the naked body of a neighboring playmate.

The incorrigible Bernard Shaw put it neatly when he argued that most child training revolves around the precept: "Don't let him!" Certainly it is true that parents and educators, in their zeal to rear tractable members of society, too often develop a compulsion to thwart the individual's fundamental nature entirely. Children are enveloped in a blanket of guilt that smothers their natural impulses to look and touch and listen. They are made to feel ashamed of their normal inquisitiveness, and are threatened with dire consequences if they exceed bounds that in most cases have been set down to suit the convenience—or the blind fears—of their adult guardians.

To the extent that civilization thus needlessly suppresses our primitive sensory activities, it diminishes our capacity to love and to achieve happiness. How can a child learn to live successfully—and to love—if he is constantly forbidden to use the very senses that are his only means of learn-

111

ing and of loving? The child cannot be expected to understand why certain objects of his investigation are "proper" and why others should be "improper." When his efforts to look or to touch are punished in any particular instance, his only possible reaction is to feel that the impulse itself is somehow wrong and therefore dangerous. The end result in most cases is not a true capacity for discrimination, but an impairment of the sensory function itself.

Here is the origin of so much of our adult timidity and lack of initiative. If so many of us live emotional lives on a starvation level of economy, it is partly because we have never shaken off the guilt attached to our earliest attempts at expressive activity. We are weighed down by the barriers placed long ago on our normal eagerness to explore the world and to immerse ourselves in its wonders. The warning finger of remembered restraint hovers constantly above us, commanding docile acceptance of pinched routines and paltry loves. We are afraid to reach out in a joyful embrace of life because, in the beginning, we were ordered to touch only that which our impatient guardians thought proper.

Sometimes our primitive senses clamor so fiercely for their long-denied outlets that they drive us into a state of rebellion. But then they can break out only in their raw, original form, subject neither to restraint nor wise direction. They emerge as criminal actions, harmful perversions, or disruptive social behavior on a mass scale.

Mankind has other alternatives and, if we will, we can save ourselves from these self-destructive extremes. Just as in government we have found that equalitarian principles of democracy may be substituted for the rule-or-ruin philosophy of a Hitlerian dictatorship, so we have learned that tolerant guidance may replace tyrannical suppression of our primitive impulses. Man does not need to be rendered blind in order that he may not covet his neighbor's wife, nor need he be made a cripple to prevent him from seizing another man's property.

There are ways in which our primitive impulses may be given adequate expression without the danger of communal anarchy. They are the ways taught by love, and we must learn them if we are to escape the catastrophes that have hitherto overwhelmed us so monotonously as individuals and as nations. It is possible to be free and happy, and at the same time to remain at peace with one another.

Nature's Academy

A sense of curiosity is nature's original school of education. Long before there were academies and institutes of technology, primitive inquisitiveness taught all the higher animals (including man) those essential details of the environment which they had to learn if they were to survive. An alert eye, a keen sense of smell, a cocked ear—these primeval teachers gave all animals their basic instruction in where to find food, how to detect enemies, when to search for a mate. An animal that failed to consult and to heed these teachers would soon be dead.

One cannot conceive of a wild creature in a state of indifference to its surroundings. Significantly, withdrawal of attention from the objects around it is almost invariably a sign that an animal is sick. As long as it remains healthy, it will be charged with a constant and insatiable curiosity, every sense quiveringly alive and straining to its utmost degree of efficiency.

Individual man, shielded by civilization against the elementary dangers of life, is ordinarily free of the need to maintain a primitive state of alertness. Yet the ways of the animal world still hold a strange fascination for us, and men periodically feel compelled to return to the exposed life of the forest and the sea. Something buried deep within us responds to the fierce concentration of the flying seagull as it darts its piercing eyes over the expanse of water in ceaseless search of food. We identify easily with the startled deer as it raises its head above the brush to listen with agonized intentness for the approach of some stealthy aggressor. The intensity with which these creatures use their sensory mechanism seems to recall a mode of existence we once shared and would strive to recapture, if only for a moment.

Behind this nostalgia is more than a mere desire for change and relaxation. Men have long begun to suspect that civilization's repression of our primitive impulses has somehow warped what are potentially the most productive forces in human nature. We are increasingly disturbed by the thought that society's passion for obedience and conformity may have overreached itself, causing us to lose in individual happiness perhaps as much as we have gained in group security. Without subscribing to Rousseau's naïve plea for a return to the "simplicity" of nature, we nevertheless feel that at least a part of civilization's restrictive design is too rigidly conceived and therefore self-defeating. There is a growing conviction that, if we are to avert a blind revolt against all social regulation, we must put into effect measures of reform that will bring psychological relief to each of us.

Civilization's stifling influence upon man's natural love of life is demonstrated daily in the subtle transformation by which the spirited child becomes the bored adult. Every normal child begins his adventure on earth with a passionate interest in everything around him, from the shape of his toes to the color of the sky. His omnivorous curiosity, like the animal's, spurs him on to a ceaseless investigation of his environment. Through this inquisitiveness he discovers both the joys and the dangers of the world in which he lives.

Success in life depends upon a continued ability to learn, and this in turn rests upon preservation of the child's original spirit of inquiry. As the Chinese proverb puts it: "He who asks a question is a fool for five minutes; he who does not ask a question remains a fool forever." Yet most of our educational methods and attitudes work to crush the child's natural curiosity the moment it exceeds conventionally defined limits. Society, placing a premium upon order and regulation, is chiefly concerned with getting the individual to *accept* the approved store of knowledge that has already been assembled. It is interested not so much in the individual's capacity to learn as in his willingness to abide by what is taught. It strives to instill precepts rather than to stimulate questions.

Education based on such an approach is really designed to *prevent* us from learning what we most need and want to know. The stultifying effect of its hostile attitude toward unconventional curiosity was vividly illustrated by an incident which occurred in the nursery school that I directed many years ago. The children at the school ranged in age from eighteen months to four years, a period of life which is crucial in the development of an individual's learning habits. At this age children have an eager, driving interest in all the basic phenomena of life. They want to know where the rain comes from, how their eliminative functions operate, why girls and boys are different.

To help me gather data on this phase of childhood, I asked one of the teachers to keep a record of the remarks made by her charges during the period when they went to the toilet. As is customary in nursery schools, the little boys and girls used the same facilities together, and I expected that their natural interest would give rise to a host of questions.

At the end of two weeks the teacher, a woman of about forty, handed me a sheet of paper on which fewer than a dozen remarks were written down. When I expressed surprise at the meagerness of the material, she assured me that she had recorded everything the children had said in her presence. Only then did it occur to me that the teacher's personality—a rather rigid one—might have affected the results.

I continued my investigation, but during the next two weeks I put in charge a young assistant who was a senior in my class at college. She was a cheerful and friendly girl, with an easy manner that endeared her to all the children. I assigned her the same task, without saying anything about the results obtained with the other teacher. This time, my aide reported back to me with a collection of more than 200 questions and remarks that the little boys and girls had spontaneously volunteered.

By traditional standards, the older of these two teachers was a thoroughly competent person in her profession. She was technically skilled in pedagogical methods, and conscientiously carried out all her duties at the school. Yet, by her unspoken attitude, she had completely stifled the eager and inquiring attitude of the children in her care. Unconsciously they knew, from the severity of her muscle tensions, that their questions would be met with embarrassment or disapproval. Her presence, in effect, made them stop trying to learn.

It is at such moments that inhibitions of lifelong duration may be placed upon the individual's free spirit of inquiry. Curiosity about the vital details of life and birth and death stems from the deepest core of the child's mind, and is the source of all his later search for knowledge. Yet questions and actions designed to obtain information about these basic matters are precisely the ones that are likely to arouse the strongest adult antagonism. The child interprets this hostile response as a sign that his own most cherished interests are somehow dangerous transgressions to be avoided at all costs. Almost automatically, he may develop a permanent pattern of concealing his curiosity or repressing it altogether.

For children will learn only in an atmosphere of love. It is the oxygen of their lives, without which all their energies are depleted and all their incentives to achievement droop

117

and fail. They will make full use of their minds and their senses only as long as they are confident that this will win them the affection of parents and teachers. They dare not risk its loss; and under the impact of adult hostility, whether open or implied, their bubbling curiosity dissolves into a murky sediment of fear and guilt. In the words of Carlyle, "Love is ever the beginning of knowledge, as fire is of light." Where there is no love, the flame of inquiry will be extinguished and dark ignorance will follow.

Sometimes the child's reaction to adult hostility may take the more positive form of deliberate rebellion against specific tasks of learning. An unconscious emotional conflict of this kind is almost invariably in the background, for example, when pupils of normal intelligence develop inexplicable blocks for certain basic subjects. Parents are likely to be very much upset when this occurs, and they often accuse the child of being "lazy" or "inattentive." A typical complaint is that the child "just won't apply himself."

Such complaints, of course, are meaningless in themselves. Behind the "laziness" may be an undetected eye defect. The child may avoid his lessons because of an unsuspected antagonism toward his teacher. Perhaps the assigned work is too difficult for his particular stage of development. The psychological background must always be explored before one can either understand or remedy the problem.

The Glory of the Senses

We Cannot Live Out Our Lives in the Lives of Our Children

I once had occasion, for example, to study an otherwise bright little boy who found it impossible to work out the elementary processes of addition and subtraction. It turned out that the boy's father was a brilliant accountant who knew mathematics instinctively and had tried to pound its principles into his son. But the boy had long harbored a strong antagonism toward his father, and it became clear that he had simply transferred this hatred onto the subject of arithmetic.

Parents often make this mistake of insisting that their children become proficient in a specific field. They try to turn their youngsters into expert golfers, scientists, musicians or some other favored choice. But this is a perilous course of action. We cannot live out our own lives in the lives of our children. They will almost invariably revolt or harbor a deep-seated resentment against us.

That is what happened with the accountant's son. It was explained to the father that he had been pushing too hard with the boy, and this had created personal antagonism between them. As soon as the father understood this, the tension was eased and the boy was able to go ahead satisfactorily in his class.

A more extreme case illustrating the same kind of disturbance occurred in one of my college classes, where an intelligent girl of nineteen proved unable to spell anything correctly. Her block in this regard was so fantastically complete that psychiatric assistance was needed before she got over it. In the course of treatment, it was discovered that after the death of her mother the little girl had been reared by an aunt who was a schoolteacher of the prim, old-fashioned type. There was much conflict between the two, and one of the things always resented by the child was the fact that her aunt continually criticized her about her spelling.

It was not difficult to draw the thread of connection. When the girl grew up, she simply used her defect as an unconscious device to express the deep antagonism she felt toward her aunt. She really took joy in her errors, for each misspelled word was for her a symbolic act of vengeance against her childhood tormentor. The block, along with other symptoms uncovered by the treatment, disappeared after the girl had worked out the problems of her original conflict.

Exaggerated symptoms like these are merely one form of reaction to the early restrictions of childhood. Far more common is the sense of boredom and futility that overtakes so many of us after we reach maturity, robbing life of its meaning and purpose. It is as if we were paralyzed by the abortive outcome of our first attempts to explore the world's mysteries, and could never again risk the danger of giving expression to our innermost desires and ambitions. Instead, we abandon our curiosity and interest, accept self-imposed limitations on our activities, and retreat into the safe cubicle of conventional routine. Like a ship with an ancient crack in the boiler, we can never permit ourselves to sail ahead at more than half-steam.

Men are often inclined to resign themselves to such a

fate, believing that life offers no other alternative. They do not realize that their sense of hopelessness and defeat is a residue of their earlier frustrations. Unconsciously they have substituted society for the parent or teacher, and once again anticipate a loss of loving approval if they step beyond the boundaries so long drawn around their minds and hearts.

Two Ways of Love

Modern psychiatry's greatest stimulus to our hope for social reform is its revelation that most of this waste in human potentialities is entirely unnecessary. Our primitive drives, it is true, must always be curbed if society is to endure. But the attempt to do so by blind suppression is not the only alternative at our command. This is merely the way of aggression, which seeks—under the sanctimonious guise of "social necessity"—to destroy the very thing it claims to preserve. It is the way that has led mankind for centuries to breed, not happy individuals, but a race of crippled victims and revengeful rebels.

Love offers us another approach. As psychiatry has discovered, man is able to control his primitive drives by deflecting them to substitute paths whenever their original goal may prove socially disruptive. To attempt a suppression of those drives is not necessary, nor can it succeed. Man's true salvation lies in his infinite capacity *to make a choice among alternatives*—that divine gift which distinguishes him from the rest of the animal world.

Love or Perish

Two basic psychological devices enable us to make such a choice. One is called the mechanism of *reaction-formation*. It teaches us to transform a destructive primitive drive into one that is directly *opposite* in character. The second device is known as displacement, or *sublimation*. Sublimation allows us to gratify a primitive drive more or less in its original form, but teaches us to choose a substitute path that will lead to a socially acceptable object or goal.

The way of reaction-formation is clearly illustrated by the nursery training which teaches children habits of cleanliness. The child is naturally an unclean creature, in the sense that it has no feeling of disgust and (left to itself) would be perfectly content to live in what adults consider unbearable conditions. But civilization demands cleanliness and sanitation, and one of the mother's first tasks is therefore to develop in the child a desire that is directly opposite to its natural impulse. *To please the mother and retain her love,* the child heeds her admonitions not to soil himself. He learns to accept the usual standards of cleanliness willingly, and in time develops the reaction-formation of disgust toward the dirt that formerly gave him pleasure. The new emotional attitude, in other words, is built up as a dam that holds back the opposite attitude from which it came.

Significantly, it is only when the mother does this with love that the reaction-formation is successfully carried out. By this I mean that the mother must approach her task calmly and without undue stress. She may encourage the child by saying he is a "good boy," or by giving him a smile of approval. She will not treat his failures as a catastrophe, nor show by her muscle tensions that she is particularly worried or displeased.

The child will then almost automatically relinquish his original pleasure in order to gain the immeasurably greater one of his mother's love. A permanent association of the two is thus established, and the reaction-formation becomes habitual and effective.

Children who are severely punished and browbeaten, on the other hand, may never give up their primitive pleasure in dirt and its psychological equivalence. In later life they will unconsciously seek symbolic means of soiling themselves and others. This may take the form of neurotic disease, stubborn and aggressive character traits, or destructive behavior patterns whose unconscious motive is to corrupt and besmirch. On the opposite plane, the reaction may take the form of overcleanliness or overconscientiousness. Those who have lived in New England farmhouses, for example, may recall how tidy housewives used to "put up" the kitchen sink at eight o'clock in the evening, after which hour no one dared get a drink of water.

Successful reaction-formations are the indispensable basis for a true social morality. Human beings are born with a basic indifference to the needs and sufferings of others. Thus one may often observe very small children standing on the street in complete calm and unconcern while they watch another child being unmercifully beaten by a stronger opponent. Children have to be taught through love to identify with their fellows and to develop mutual consideration through the reaction-formation of sympathy.

Many of our basic legal, religious and humanitarian principles are developed through the same mechanism. Respect for private property is learned only as a reaction-formation against man's original impulse to seize and appropriate whatever lies in his path. The humanitarian who crusades for the prevention of cruelty to animals may have started as a child who took delight in torturing his pet kitten. Saint Paul's famous conversion to Christianity was simply a reaction-formation against his earlier career of excessive cruelty to Christ's followers.

Sublimation—the second way of love—is the road followed by the eternally creative spirit of man. It offers us the most constructive method of turning a primitive impulse from undesirable objectives to useful and pleasurable activities. Through it, humanity is able to augment the joy of life, obtaining compensation for the loss of the natural state it once shared with the rest of the animal kingdom.

The way of sublimation may be illustrated by tracing the various paths that may be taken by our primitive impulse to look. The sense of sight is an automatic function of the eye and ordinarily is allowed full freedom. But it also plays a large role in gratifying sexual curiosity, and here children are met with severe restrictions. In civilized life, concealment of nudity and of sexual activities is more or less complete. The restriction is sharpest when it comes to the child's original curiosity, which is directed toward the parents as one of its first objects of interest.

The ultimate path taken by this primitive impulse to look depends on the manner in which it is turned aside from its original objects. If it is met simply with harsh suppression and punishment, it may become in later life the basis for serious disturbances of various kinds. Because of overpowering guilt attached to it, for example, it often is the source of functional diseases of the eye. On a neurotic level, it may result in the phenomenon of the Peeping Tom. As a distorted behavior trait, it may appear in the guise of the snooper who takes delight in gossiping about his neighbors. Sometimes the reaction against the original curiosity may be so intense that on an intellectual level it produces exactly opposite traits. Such is the case with the obstructionist, who blindly opposes education, popular enlightenment and freedom of thought.

If the original impulse is instead encouraged to choose substitute interests, then the path of sublimation lies open before us. Such is the road taken, for example, by the scientist who penetrates by microscope and telescope into the mysteries of nature. The energy derived from the primitive drive of his original curiosity is now sublimated into his passion for research. Where once he could not investigate the mysteries of sexual activity, he now examines the behavior of the microbe and plots the course of the stars.

Mankind's greatest scientific achievements may be described as sublimations of the primitive impulse to look. It was curiosity, usefully and pleasurably employed, which led Leeuwenhoek to invent the first microscope—and thus to discover the "little beasties," or bacteria, that cause disease. The great English physician, William Harvey, spent long hours watching the beating hearts of animals, and so learned the secret of the circulation of the blood. Unquenchable curiosity drove Vesalius to steal skeletons from the gallows, and thus gave the world the facts of human anatomy.

Love or Perish

Sublimation offers an endless variety of possible substitutes to gratify our primitive curiosity. They range from art and astronomy to photography and surveying. But the path of sublimation can be successfully reached only if the child is led to it through loving tolerance and guidance. "There is a power in love," wrote Emerson, "to divine another's destiny better than that other can, and, by heroic encouragement, hold him to his task." How many of us are cheated of our destiny because, instead, our budding interests were ruthlessly cast aside or contemptuously ignored!

I remember visiting the summer home of a friend of mine whose young son was very much interested in snakes. It was a startling experience to enter that house, for reptiles of many sizes and varieties literally crawled all over the place. The boy had built homes for the creatures in various locations around the house, and you never knew whether or not a snake would suddenly appear from under the chair or come sliding over the window sill. They were harmless, nonpoisonous specimens, of course. Still, not all visitors could be expected to enjoy their company.

Boys often develop such interests, but ordinarily parents dismiss these as childish nonsense or ban them altogether as impossible nuisances. Certainly, few parents would tolerate the invasion of their home by an army of snakes. In this instance, however, both parents had a sympathetic background, for the father was a professor of anatomy and the mother a teacher of biology. They encouraged the boy in his unique interest, and at the age of fourteen he wrote a monograph on reptilian habits that won him a national scientific award. Today he is a research scientist doing notable work in the field of animal biology.

The Glory of the Senses

The Joy of Life

Once we accept the ways of love, there is no end to the opportunities that lie before us for joyful living. Love permits the adult the free use of his imagination and his sensory powers. It enables him to recapture the naïve delight of the round-eyed child absorbed in the wonders of a stone, a cat, a mud pie. It releases the burdens of old prohibitions, renewing an attitude of open curiosity that seeks eagerly for knowledge of the world and its ways.

There is no end of new things, all within arm's length, to explore and to assimilate. How many of us understand the principles of stress on which our own homes are built? How many of us can describe the habits of the insects in our back yard? Birds fly over us all our lives—how many of us are familiar with the mysterious and fascinating migratory cycle that brings them back each spring?

Yet these things are right around us, forming an essential part of everyday life. It is not necessary to climb Mt. Everest or to fly to the moon in order to enrich our lives. We have but to move one unaccustomed step forward, to open one unfamiliar book, to lift our eyes from the ground to the sky—and a host of thrilling novelties appears to enkindle our minds and souls.

Love teaches us that we must go forward and embrace what we would possess. Happiness does not come to us of its own accord. Neither is it a prize to be won only through lucky lotteries. The capacity for joy resides in the constant use of our senses, our muscles, our minds. It comes from within ourselves, and must be made an habitual part of our daily activity.

In this sense, we can all be in a constant state of love! Let a man dedicate himself to hunting out all the new things that his eyes can see, and he will find fascination throughout the years. There is delight in listening to the whine of the wind, the humming of insects, the echo of the waterfall, the ripple of the lake. There is joy in the smooth texture of a leaf, the crunching of earth under foot. There is humor in the snoring of a dog, the twist of a bird's head, the flick of a cat's tail.

These and a thousand and one other things make the world a marvelous place, filled with ceaseless wonders that a man may love to the end of his days.

CHAPTER SEVEN

With Loving Hands

M AN is a muscular organism whose destiny, though shaped by dreams and desires, is achieved only through action taken in a world of reality. We are all kings and conquerors in the silent empire of our fantasies; and there was once a moment, at the dawn of infancy, when we were content to accept such illusory triumphs as the true measure of our happiness. But nature, embedding itself in the very structure of our bodies, propels us irresistibly forward to express its primitive drives in concrete deeds. The human mechanism is animated by nerves and muscles which atrophy if not used, and only through their ceaseless function is it possible to obtain our abiding satisfactions. In the biological sense, man is a creature that must move and act in order to live.

Yet there is another set of forces that imposes equally relentless pressures upon the ultimate course of human conduct. Though the drive to action springs originally from the internal chemistry of our cells, life can be maintained only if in addition we draw love and sustenance from the world outside. All human activity is thus set to spinning under the sway of a dual compulsion. We must accommodate ourselves to the demands of the community, or we die for lack of food and protection. We must also obey the living organism's inexorable need to function in accord with its own, mysterious nature, else we shrivel and suffocate from the emotional poisons of self-frustration.

Success in life depends upon the individual's ability to reconcile these two imperious claims upon our energies. One may even view the history of the race as a record of the repeated struggle to find a compromise. Yet it is precisely this requirement which sets mankind upon a seemingly impossible task! For the biological fact remains that *all human effort involves aggression*. To do anything at all, we must use the muscular apparatus of our bodies—and muscular energy, in its primitive form, is basically *aggressive* energy. How can a human being work in co-operation with others, how can he sacrifice even a portion of his energy for constructive purposes, when the very physiology of his body seems to dictate an exclusively aggressive path of action?

We face this psychological dilemma a hundred times a day. Almost everything we do, for example, involves the use of our hands. Ordinarily we think of the human hand as a delicate and wonderfully skillful instrument. A study of its structure and mode of operation, however, reveals that it is actually a modified kind of talon. Despite evolutionary development, the human hand still remains essentially what it was in primitive times—an aggressive mechanism designed to seize and grasp, to rip and scratch, to squeeze, push and strike.

Long centuries of culture have not removed the need to use these primitive, aggressive actions even in the most innocuous of our daily tasks. When a farmer gathers fruit from a tree, the muscular performance is intrinsically the same as that of the predatory savage in the ancient forest. When a mechanic twists an engine bolt into place, he uses the same primitive force our forebears employed to wring the neck of a hapless bird caught for the next meal. And one need only observe the grasp-reflex of a newborn baby to realize how closely bound we are, from the beginning, to these primordial patterns of action. Barrie's intuitive symbolization of our aggressive heritage was correct when, in *Peter Pan,* he gave the murderous Captain Hook an iron claw for a hand.

Modern man thus moves through a civilized world with the muscular equipment nature gave us for self-preservation in a tooth-and-claw environment. It is from this basic contradiction that some of our most oppressive psychological burdens arise. Unconsciously, our muscles yearn to follow the path of aggressive action for which they were originally designed. Consciously, we are called upon to deny their primitive course and deflect our aims toward constructive social goals. One inevitable consequence is that a part of our energy must be marshaled against our own natural drives even as we strive to use it for conquering life's external obstacles. It is as if a prize fighter were permitted to enter the ring only on condition that he improve the health of his opponent!

But another and even more oppressive burden stems

from our own internal reaction to the conflicting demands of society. It takes the form of a sense of guilt, and it is developed because of the realization that *man can never eliminate the aggressive origin of his energy*. We remain subtly and constantly aware of this inexorable fact as long as we continue to use the muscles of our bodies. Few of us entirely escape the ensuing sense of guilt, and for many it becomes a leaden anchor of inhibition that is dragged through all of life's activities.

The problem thus imposed by civilization becomes especially burdensome in the daily work to which most of us devote a major portion of our lives. For it is here, in the very nature of our pursuits, that we draw most actively upon the store of aggressive energy within ourselves. We cannot till the soil, build houses, dig wells or operate machines without an unimpeded flow of sheer physical force. If we are entrepreneurs, we cannot survive the intense economic competition and personal rivalries of the business world without putting forth a full measure of aggressive effort. Nor can society itself afford to stop this flood of primitive power, since that is the source of its own ability to sustain and protect its members.

It is clear that we can neither release nor control this power effectively so long as men are compelled to labor under the double burden of internal guilt and external coercion. A sense of guilt may cripple our muscular efforts as effectively as any organic disease. It can paralyze our initiative, limit our ambition, hobble our skills. At the very least, it will destroy the confidence without which no one can derive full satisfaction from his work.

With Loving Hands

External coercion, on the other hand, deprives us of a meaningful goal for our efforts. This is no less true in contemporary society than it was, for example, in feudal times. We are no longer personal slaves, but work has increasingly become a kind of soulless tyranny in itself. Under modern industrial conditions, more and more people find that they have little genuine interest in what they do. They are but tiny cogs, as a rule, in a huge machine directed by remote corporate management. Work has become specialized and fragmented to the point where it carries little intrinsic significance, and the worker himself is turned into an anonymous treadle for someone else to step upon. He thereby loses both his personal identity and his sense of humanity. He simply puts in his "time" on the job, almost like a prisoner, and his only reward is the weekly paycheck which is dangled over his head like a whip to keep him in line.

Men and women need more than a salary to make life worth while. When work is not a source of personal satisfaction, it fails to serve as a proper outlet for our aggressive energy. That is why so many of us go through our jobs with a sense of futility or depression. That is partly the reason, too, for the widespread symptoms of anxiety so characteristic of modern times. It is difficult to get angry at a corporation or a holding company. One is left simply with a general feeling of frustration. This stirs uneasily all through society, and it is an explosive reservoir of resentment which must not be underestimated in its potential capacity for destruction.

Our solution for this problem can be found in only one

direction. We must devise methods, specifically, that will teach us how to accept our aggressive energy as a *normal* and *inevitable* part of life. We must learn how to use this energy *freely* and *confidently,* without a sense of guilt. And, finally, we must find an inner motive that will lead men to direct this energy toward constructive goals *voluntarily,* instead of through external compulsion.

We must find an answer, in brief, that will enable men and women to become loving masters, not resentful victims, of the powerful life forces within themselves.

The Carpenter's Miracle

Fortunately, there is a marvelous creative force that man generates within himself as an antidote to his own destructive drives. That creative antidote takes a specific form. It arises as *an unconscious impulse in man to make reparation —to restore what we would destroy.*

The impulse to make reparation is a form of love, and appears within our hearts at the very beginning of life. It flows as a direct consequence of the newborn infant's aggressive reactions to the separation from the mother and to the inevitable delays in the gratification of its needs. The infant's outbursts of rage (as we have seen) are of primitive violence, and in fantasy the child destroys the "bad" mother who has caused all its deprivations and sufferings. But the child cannot survive without the mother's love and protection. Its destructive fantasy leaves the infant with a terrible sense of loss and danger, and unconsciously it is driven to remedy the intolerable situation. Again in fantasy, the child now re-creates the "destroyed" mother and restores her, intact, to her former presence. Its hostile emotions subside, and once more the child feels safe and secure with the beneficent mother, source of all that is valuable in life.

This profound and momentous infantile experience remains indelibly engraved upon our unconscious mind. It becomes a prototype of emotional response that may be repeated over and over again throughout our lives in actual or symbolic form. Whenever we are again filled with angry or destructive impulses, we unconsciously experience the same sense of danger—the same fear that we will lose the love and protection we need in order to live. And again we are moved to make amends. If we have literally caused offense or injury, we hasten to repair the damage by apologies, gifts, payments, or actual physical reconstruction. If our destructiveness has occurred on an unconscious emotional plane, we make reparation by symbolically restoring the victims of our aggressions and thus winning back the love we have lost. The sculptor who models a beautiful statue, for example, is often motivated by an unconscious desire to re-create the "lost" mother.

The impulse to make reparation may express itself in many aspects of human life. We see it in a clear form when the people of warring nations unite after peace comes and contribute funds to rebuild a beautiful cathedral destroyed during the hostilities. It is a fundamental element in the pleasure obtained from many types of play activity—as when a child builds a house of blocks, knocks them down with a crash, and then laboriously puts them together again, to repeat the cycle indefinitely. Adults derive a similar kind of pleasure when they spend hours fitting jigsaw puzzles together.

A more subtle manifestation is the sense of responsibility and the regard for others that we develop as we grow into maturity. Concern for the welfare of other people shows that we have mastered our aggressive feelings toward them and are worthy of their love and co-operation. That is usually why, for example, we participate in charity drives or join business and social organizations. The same motive plays a large part in our desire to become good fathers and mothers to our children. By acting as good parents ourselves, we give tangible proof to the world that we have made reparation for the aggressive feelings we once had toward our own parents. The impulse to make amends thus serves as a basic tool in our efforts to establish harmonious human relationships.

Yet there is an even more significant role that the mechanism of reparation can play in the fate of mankind as a whole. Potentially, it is the solution men seek in their struggle with the basic dilemma of civilization. It is the instrument that can teach us how to cope with the unbridled aggressions and chronic discontents that have so disrupted the stability of modern society. For within its psychological pattern lies the secret from which men can learn how to perform their daily work in joy and loving co-operation.

The secret is in itself not difficult to discover. We see it clearly revealed, for example, in the task performed by a carpenter when he builds a house. Like all other men, carpenters work in order to earn money for the necessities of life. But that is far from the whole story. The construction of a house is also a complex human experience that sets into motion a variety of profound psychological forces. It involves, to begin with, a series of highly aggressive and even destructive acts. Living trees must be chopped down to supply wood, and this must again be hacked and sawed into smaller pieces. Planks must be nailed together with violent hammer blows. Surfaces must be scraped and cut with a plane, and joints gouged out with ruthless strokes of the chisel.

Despite the intensely aggressive character of these actions, the carpenter is able to derive deep satisfaction from his labors. He is free to use his muscular energy in primitive form without incurring a sense of guilt. But he is able to do this—to obtain untrammeled gratification from his work—only because his ultimate goal from the start is to reassemble the destroyed parts into a new home that others will use and admire. He has an added incentive to press forward with his work because his reward, apart from money, will include social approval and gratitude for his specific accomplishment.

If we stop to consider the nature of that accomplishment in human terms, we will see that the carpenter has done more than merely build a house. He has found a successful way, in symbolic form, to carry out the infantile fantasy of destroying and then re-creating the "lost" mother. Psychologically, he has worked a miracle: he has of his own volition transformed his primitive, aggressive energy into love, and this in turn has won back the spontaneous love of his fellow men!

Here, in the "carpenter's miracle," is the compromise men seek in their immemorial struggle with the opposing forces of love and aggression. For all human work is in the deepest sense an attempt to find a balanced outlet for the primitive energies that swirl and clash within us. Men and women do not look upon work merely as a means of earning a livelihood, nor simply as a technique for manufacturing essential goods. They universally invest it with a symbolic meaning, and react to it as something that either gratifies or denies their unconscious emotional needs. Work becomes a major drama of life, and the plot is brought to a happy ending when the fantasy of reparation is successfully played out.

All work takes on this symbolic aspect, regardless of its nature. The farmer, for example, rips deep furrows into the ground as he digs it up with his plough; but he compensates for his destructive action by growing food which will nourish and "restore" human life. The tailor cuts cloth up into useless little pieces, only to sew them together again into beautiful garments that will both adorn and protect human beings. The worker at a blast furnace burns and melts down valuable mineral ore, but re-forms it into steel girders that become the sturdy skeletons of new and useful buildings. And the forester who labors to prevent destruction of our natural resources is in fantasy preserving the real mother symbolized in Mother Nature.

Viewed in this light, all work becomes essentially a

search for love. By the same token, work can never serve the true purposes of man or society *unless it is primarily rewarded with love.* The whole mechanism of reparation is originally set in motion because man has both a profound fear of losing love and an insatiable desire to regain it. At first this is experienced in the form of a fantasy, but through work it is later played out as actual deeds in a world of reality. Man therefore succeeds in making reparation—that is, he successfully transforms aggression into love—only if two realistic conditions are present. His work must allow him to feel that he is creating something new and good as a replacement for the lost mother. And he must win loving approval from his fellow men, as an individual, for carrying out his creative deed.

Modern industry commits a basic psychological error when it fails to provide these conditions for the individual worker. Businessmen of imagination know this and are trying to do something about it. In his recent book, *Are Workers Human?*, Gordon R. Taylor tells of an experiment in an English factory that produced hearing aids for the deaf. Ordinarily, a team of ten girls carried out the assembly and wiring of these devices, with each girl limited to a single operation. In the experiment, one of the girls volunteered to try to carry out all ten operations by herself.

At first, as she learned the different steps, her rate of work slowed up. But within six months she was able to produce complete units at a rate *twice that of the average output of the team.* In other words, the interest and satisfaction generated by the complete creative process enabled her to accomplish as much as two girls did on the assembly line.

Similar experiments elsewhere, as cited by Taylor, show clearly that modern industrial conditions produce profound frustration in the lives of most workers. The anxieties that follow affect not only individual happiness, but also industrial output. Both happiness and output increase when the workers are given incentive, prestige and a sense of accomplishment as rewards for their labor.

That, in brief, is the psychological formula society must apply to the basic problem of controlling man's aggressions. Each of us must be allowed to perform the carpenter's miracle. Each of us must be encouraged to win success in acting out the fantasy of reparation. For this alone meets the specifications we have found to be essential if mankind is to preserve its stability in a world threatened on every side by the forces of destruction. This is the secret alchemy by which man can accept his aggressive drives without guilt, and transform them voluntarily into the creative action that binds us together with mutual love and respect.

Love Excels

Some years ago, one of the nation's largest industrial corporations opened a large branch factory in the Middle West. A company executive told me with pride of the extensive measures they had taken to make the new factory a model of comfort and efficiency. High-priced architects had conducted elaborate surveys to determine what type of building design would best meet the workers' needs. Engineers had been engaged especially to devise new, accident-proof machines. Millions of dollars were spent to make the factory air-conditioned and dust-free.

But not one cent was spent by the corporation to make a study of the people who would work in its factory! No one made the slightest effort beforehand to discover a single fact about their personalities, their hopes and ambitions, their problems as human beings!

Behind that incident lies one of the fundamental psychological errors of modern industrial society. It is the tacit belief, widely held throughout the business and economic world, that work is primarily a physical activity to be dealt with in purely physical terms. It is the false view that a worker is simply an instrument of material energy, who makes material things, for which in return he earns a material reward. As a corollary to this view, a successful society is assumed to be one that will provide the maximum material gains in these three divisions of the economic structure. It will be one that gives physical employment to the greatest possible number of people, produces the maximum quantity of material goods, and yields the largest possible payment in material rewards.

Well-meaning economists confidently present this goal as an enlightened blueprint for human happiness. And yet such a program by itself is an invitation to social disaster. It ignores the basic psychological truth that physical energy is primarily aggressive energy, and can express itself only along destructive paths if it is not mixed with love. The material view of work makes the dangerous assumption that men can be prevailed upon by physical means alone to labor toward constructive ends. It fails to realize that the twin forces of love and aggression cannot be separated except at the peril of losing life itself.

Psychiatrists see this truth demonstrated every day in their study of the criminal and the neurotic. What is the actual offense, for example, of the vandal who defaces a public park by destroying trees and shrubbery? His physical actions are intrinsically no different from those of the carpenter who builds a house. The distinction lies in the different goals to which these actions are directed. The carpenter, motivated by love and the desire to win love, turns his efforts to a loving and useful purpose. The vandal—either because of a hostile early background or a constitutional inability to receive love—has never developed the indispensable motive for controlling his aggressions. His emotional fantasies stop at the image of the "bad" mother or father. He never passes the emotional stage of frustration and rage, for he has been left permanently without hope or desire of ever winning love. The public park is merely a symbol of the wicked society upon which he must wreak his anger. Without love to guide his hand, he has no reason to use his energies for anything but destruction.

Only the criminal dissociates love and aggression to such a pathological extreme. But all of us are subject to emotional disturbances that come from a partial or temporary failure to fuse the two in equal balance.

With Loving Hands

One of my patients, for example, was a salesman who came to me for treatment because of difficulties in his work. Curiously enough, his symptoms had been brought on by success rather than failure. He found that after making a sale he would go into a state of anxiety and depression. Sometimes he would be left so exhausted that he was incapable of doing anything at all, and he would remain in bed for days at a time before he was able to resume his work.

My patient represented a company that manufactured a superior type of labor-saving machine, and actually his work provided a definite service to people. Nevertheless he came to view each successful sale either as a deprivation inflicted upon some rival salesman, or as an attack upon the customer. "I feel as if I were robbing the customer," he explained to me, "instead of selling him something he needs."

Our analysis revealed that the patient had formerly been in business with a dominating partner whose behavior was that of a severe father-figure. He had chafed under this domination and had finally left to go into business for himself. In his success as a salesman, however, he came to feel that he was displacing his father, with whom he had been in great conflict as a child. Each sale became a guilty act of aggression. It was in fantasy an attack upon his father; and unconsciously he felt he should be punished for it. His symptoms of anxiety and depression, we found, were simply a form of punishment that he imposed upon himself.

Now, salesmen are peculiarly subject to this kind of de-

pression. Because business practice usually places emphasis upon the sale rather than the thing sold, salesmen tend
to view their work primarily as an act of aggression in
which they rob and injure their customers. The "dry spell"
so common among them is unconsciously a period of self-
punishment during which they can work off their sense
of guilt. As in the case of my patient, their guilt is aroused
because the element of love has been removed from their
work. My patient was cured when he overcame his infantile view of his father as a wicked parent and thus removed the unconscious source of his need to "attack" and
destroy. The world of business, on the other hand, often
encourages men to retain this aggressive view and to use
work as an instrument of power and domination.

Sometimes, it is true, work disturbances are caused by
our own failure to make proper use of love's guiding hand.
This was illustrated in the case of a surgeon, a man of 38,
who came for treatment, like the salesman, because of
painful anxieties about his work. The surgeon also had
been successful in his practice, until he developed morbid
qualms about his own medical competence. At first this
showed itself in doubts as to whether he had performed his
operations as skillfully as he might. Then he began to
worry after each operation whether he had tied up the
arteries properly, and he would awake at night with a panicky fear that his patient might have bled to death inter-
nally. His anxieties finally became so acute that he could
no longer trust himself to go on with his profession.

A study of the surgeon's history showed that in his case
the work disturbances arose from an imperfect sublima-

tion. By "sublimation" we mean that one transfers the energy of an instinctive force to a socially acceptable goal instead of its original object. At first, the surgeon had been able to do this through powerful unconscious motives to heal and restore. As a child he had a strong curiosity about his mother's internal organs, and sometimes in his anger at her he would have fantasies of cutting her up. This is a normal experience among children and ordinarily passes away. In this case, it became a strong fixation that led my patient in later life to become a surgeon by way of compensation.

His professional work thus enabled him to act out the fantasy of reparation to a successful conclusion. But in his success, he began to lose sight of his original purpose. Surgery more and more for him took on the aspects of a business rather than a healing art, until at last its function as a means of sublimation broke down. A residue of his infantile aggressive fantasies cropped up again and revived his original sense of guilt. Each operation then became for him an unconscious act of injury upon the beloved mother instead of a service of love that would restore her. With the understanding gained from analysis, he was able to fuse love with aggression once more and to resume his practice on a firm basis.

Our contemporary industrial society, far from encouraging the fusion of love with aggression, tends to place a premium upon their separation. It insists that "sentiment has no place" in business, which is another way of saying that love must be eliminated from it. Businessmen go further and maintain that the economic world is a jungle ruled by the law of "kill or be killed." Even when they are moved by a loving attitude toward their work, they are ashamed to acknowledge it for fear it will be interpreted as a sign of weakness. They feel they can prove their competence only if they act in a driving and ruthless manner toward competitor, associate and employee alike. Their goal becomes exclusively one of beating the other fellow, of winning ever more power and money.

Such a view seeks to divide life into separate parts. It makes work primarily a channel for aggression, and reserves the rewards of love for moments of relaxation and leisure. But life cannot be so compartmentalized. Life is all of one piece. Men err when they think they can be inhuman exploiters in their business life, and loving husbands and fathers at home. For achievement without love is a cold and tight-lipped murderer of human happiness everywhere. It produces only *things,* and never human bonds. Since it thrives by releasing the cruel forces of aggression, it can breed only guilt and hate in return. Ultimately it strikes down the businessman himself with heart attacks, or nephritis, or paralyzing depressions while he is still young. And usually its destructive effects also engulf those whom we would love.

This is not to say that men must renounce their aggressive drives entirely. On the contrary, such an attempt would be foolish in the extreme, for it would deprive us of the dynamo that supplies our creative energy in the first place. The man who tries to live by love alone exposes himself to annihilation by all the hostile forces that nature itself has planted on earth. Such a person is like the all-

With Loving Hands

loving, all-understanding, all-sacrificing Prince Myshkin of Dostoyevski's famous novel—an epileptic "idiot" who is in the end destroyed by his own infinite goodness. It is a matter of balance between the forces of love and aggression, not their mutual exclusion. The destiny of love is to *guide* the forces of aggression so that life—vigorous, active, competitive life—may be preserved.

The harassed industrial executive struggling to dominate his self-created jungle is likely to turn a pitying smile toward such claims for love. Yet economic history itself shows that men win their greatest victories when they infuse love into their work. Americans performed miracles of industrial productivity during the last war, shattering all previous records, only because they were united in a loving purpose—in this case, the love and preservation of their mother country. The very machines responsible for industry in the first place were created by inventors and scientists whose achievements grew directly out of intense love for their work. It was Pasteur's loving devotion to chemical research that saved France's wine industry. The modern miracle of aviation, again, is due solely to love. The Wright brothers toiled for years with infinite patience and little material reward, because of their passion for flying. In his autobiography, *The Spirit of St. Louis,* Charles A. Lindbergh dwells on his early love of the air, of his love for the sky and the sensation of flying through the mysterious firmament. It was creative love that alone persuaded these pioneers to persist until the victorious end. Love, in short, here created an art, a science and an industry where nothing existed before.

147

Love or Perish

Thus does man's love have power to change the world, to bend the shape of reality to fit the bias of his fantasy. The poets have long known this secret. In the noble lines of Longfellow:

Ah, how skillful grows the hand
That obeyeth Love's command!
It is the heart, and not the brain,
That to the highest doth attain,
And he who followeth Love's behest
Far excelleth all the rest!

No man can win true happiness unless he learns to work with loving hands. No society can endure unless it permits its members to work the miracle of love in their daily tasks, on however small a scale. "Blessed is he who has found his work; let him ask no other blessedness," wrote Carlyle in profound recognition of this eternal truth. Our task must be to see that each man, in his own way, is so blessed.

CHAPTER EIGHT

The Impatient Heart

O<small>URS</small> is a logical world, where men must have rational motives to justify their actions. But the human personality, like the ancient god Janus, is a twin-faced entity under whose sway our sympathies stretch in two opposite directions at once. Outwardly we turn the solemn mien of reason and agree to base our conduct on the laws of cause and effect that govern reality. Inwardly we wear the wild visage of emotion and refuse to recognize either time or circumstance as master. It is because of this dual dominion that our relationships to others in everyday life so often become hopelessly confused and destructive.

Wisdom cautions us that we cannot truly judge another's character and personality until we have observed his behavior over an extended period of time. "A man must eat a peck of salt with his friend, before he knows him," declared Cervantes long ago. Despite this, we never meet a strange person without experiencing an immediate emotional reaction that may range in intensity from casual dislike to enthusiastic admiration. It does not matter whether the stranger is a sales clerk, a candidate for Congress, or the new boss of the firm. We never remain neutral in attitude—at least in the unconscious—but in every case form an instant opinion based on our automatic emotional response.

Dim memories of prehistoric times, when primitive man had to be constantly on the alert for potential enemies, may partly account for these initial reactions. But in civilized life they are based largely on our own past experiences and often have nothing to do with the actual circumstances of the present. They stem largely from our private stronghold of emotions, where quantities of love and hate have been secretly stored up from earliest years as a supply to be used all through later life. Since the impatient heart of man cannot always wait for fortune to favor its cause, we often tap this reservoir upon the slightest pretext and pour out love or hate without regard for ultimate consequences. In this respect our emotions erupt like creeping vines, which must reach out and attach themselves to whatever object they may find nearby.

A chain of error and conflict may thus be set in motion from the very moment that people meet. For we rarely admit, either to others or to ourselves, that our judgments have been determined by our own secret emotional needs. Instead, we defer to the laws of logic and find plausible excuses for our conduct. And it is always easy to do this. All people have both virtues and vices, and we need but seize upon one or another trait to justify our conclusions about them. We magnify these traits, or invent other faults at will to suit our preconceived attitudes, until the true origin of our behavior is permanently lost to view. In the end we become hopelessly enmeshed in a web of false complications from which we cannot extricate ourselves except at the cost of bitterness and disillusion. If this happens in a major relationship, such as marriage or a business partnership, our whole existence may be turned into a thing of misery and ruin.

Everyday life abounds in familiar examples of the way in which all of us use transparent excuses to give vent to our private emotions. The vice-president of a corporation, resentful because the board of directors has failed to vote him an overdue increase in salary, angrily threatens to fire the department supervisor who appears ten minutes late with a sales report. The supervisor, smarting under the unjustified rebuke, takes his wife severely to task at home when he finds the roast slightly overcooked. Chagrined by her husband's reprimand, the wife upbraids their little son for leaving his toys on the floor. The boy, resentful of his mother's harshness, scolds the household dog because it has chewed on a new rubber ball.

In this miniature cycle of unhappiness lies the clue to much of the havoc wrought in human relationships everywhere. Each person in the cycle has been made the scapegoat for an offense committed by someone else. Each has had just cause for anger, but at every link in the chain the emotion has been stifled at its point of origin. A trivial pretext has then been seized upon at the first opportunity, and the pent-up emotion has been transferred, or "displaced," onto an innocent victim. *At no point in the cycle of hostility has the emotional expression been justified by the actual circumstances of the moment.*

In brief, it is the *misdirection* of our emotions, not the emotions themselves, that leads us astray in our dealings with other people. Honest disagreement and open conflict based on realistic issues are a normal part of life. They may be said to have a salutary effect, for they compel us to resolve a problem definitely one way or another and thus dissipate the charged emotional attitudes that may surround it.

Sometimes our very survival requires that we come out and vigorously oppose the tyrannical or corrupt men who would destroy what we hold most dear. Few of us would today lead free lives, for example, had not the Allied nations summoned all of their strength to combat the monstrous attack upon civilization launched by Hitler and his Nazi legions. In the same way, when an insane man runs amok with a loaded gun down a crowded street, our only recourse may be to kill him. Nor can we remain complacent when drug peddlers prey upon young children, or when ignoble demagogues pervert their high office for personal aggrandizement. We would be remiss if we did not experience indignation on such occasions and move with all our resources to remedy the evil. We must hate evil—but not the evil-doer. He should be understood or, if possible, helped.

The damage is done when we bury our honest anger, allow it to fester in secret, and then permit it to erupt as virulent and aimless hate. In this chronic form, it can attain only the distorted expression of cruelty and injustice. It provokes only pointless quarrels, irreparable breaches, disastrous self-defeats. Since it has no real goal other than its own self-perpetuation, it thrives on misunderstandings and avoids all solutions or compromises in human relationships. Unchecked, its course leads inevitably to destruction.

The Masks of Hostility

The first step in the correction of this basic psychological error clearly must be the recognition of the concealed forces that produce it. Chronic hostility wears many masks. Some are only slightly twisted in the grimace they present to the world. Thus, we all have our favorite prejudices—perhaps a dislike of cats, an antipathy toward members of the opposite political party, or an abiding aversion for the sound of the saxophone. None of these may be based on justifiable grounds, yet they do no great harm and need not cause much concern.

It is the more deeply distorted masks of hostility that inspire the wearer to deeds of irreparable evil. These are the malignant faces of religious bigotry, hatred of minority groups, class antagonism—all forms of misdirected hate that may easily lead, as in the past, to barbarous persecutions and devastating wars. Where only our own personal relationships are involved, they may drive us forward upon utterly senseless paths of behavior ending in ruin either to others or to ourselves.

153

Love or Perish

A dramatic instance of such a denouement occurred in a Boston restaurant several years ago. It took place one evening after a young man had quietly given the waiter his order for a light supper which included a portion of baked beans. When the meal came, the patron discovered that brown bread had been served with the beans instead of the white bread he had ordered. He rose in a sudden burst of rage, seized the waiter by the throat, and would have strangled him to death had not several other patrons pried him loose after a violent struggle.

One might dismiss this grotesque act as simply the product of a deranged mind. After the young man had been arrested, however, a court psychiatrist uncovered the distorted background that led to the assault. It turned out that the young man had been captured during the war and held for more than a year in a German prison camp. There he had to subsist on a diet whose main dish was a thin soup, made of potatoes and half-spoiled meat, and served with coarse brown bread of which about twenty per cent was bran. He was a husky six-footer who weighed 170 pounds when he entered the prison camp, but the near-starvation diet had reduced him to 100 pounds by the time he was liberated.

In that Boston restaurant, the waiter's trivial error revived the memory of the whole bitter experience. All his pent-up rage toward his German captors rose at sight of the brown bread, and the "displaced" fury was turned against the waiter who had unwittingly brought him the hated diet.

Most persons acquire sufficient self-control in life to prevent violent outbreaks of this kind. Yet all of us are often

154

motivated in our behavior by the same kind of distorted emotional attitudes toward friends or strangers. Our actions, if less spectacular, are equally false, and in the long run may prove just as destructive. They may result, for example, in the kind of breakdown that overtook an air force captain whom I was asked to see not long after the close of the last war. He was a college graduate, an honor man who had served with distinction both during the war and with the occupation forces afterward in Germany. He was slated for promotion to the rank of lieutenant colonel, but on his return to this country he suddenly went AWOL and disappeared for several months. He wandered aimlessly around the country, worked at odd jobs in various cities, and was finally picked up after he had passed several bad checks.

Here, again, a plausible description like "combat fatigue" might have been used to explain away the captain's irresponsible conduct. But a deeper motive seemed indicated as soon as I learned that the captain's father, himself a high-ranking military officer, had refused to intervene on the son's behalf. The older man could have taken several steps in a legitimate effort to forestall the court-martial that loomed ahead. Instead he chose to adopt a stiff, official attitude, and he remained aloof from the entire affair even though his son's future career was at stake.

After several interviews with the captain, the true origin of his self-destructive course began to be apparent. The father, it developed, had always been a martinet. Rigid and unbending, he had harshly disciplined his son from childhood on. The boy had outwardly accepted this au-

155

thority, to the extent that he became a model military man himself. But inwardly he smoldered with a lifelong resentment whose existence he himself would have been the first to deny. When the buried hatred could no longer be contained, it erupted in the masked form of rebellion against military discipline rather than in open defiance of his father. The ruin of his own fortunes, since it would also bring disgrace to the older officer, was a disguised act of revenge.

Now it may be plausibly argued that life itself gives us all good reason to harbor resentment and to seek revenge. After all, the world *is* full of injustice and unprovoked evil. There *are* tyrants and scoundrels who do us injury through no fault of our own. Even in the normal course, we were all subjected as children to oppressions and indignities against which we had no redress. Parents frustrated our legitimate wishes, older brothers or sisters bullied us into painful submission, younger members of the family received favored treatment. As we went out into the world, few of us escaped being exploited at times by dishonest and merciless men. We may have been cheated out of our money, denied a promotion because of jealous intrigues, deserted in a crisis by a trusted friend. In view of these universal cruelties, it may be asked, how can any of us hope to be free of secret hate?

One may acknowledge the truth of these facts and yet point to a profound fallacy in the conclusion drawn from them. The question is not whether secret hate is justified, but whether it does us any good. Depth psychology reveals, on the contrary, that chronic hate can lead us only into fatal errors. Under its goading, *we invariably mistake the present for the past.* We are not aware of the true motive for our actions, because the original cause has been buried in the unconscious and forgotten. To justify our behavior, we are therefore compelled to invent new causes that we pluck out of the air and substitute for the old. We become convinced that our resentments are now due to the present evils done to us, when all the while we are driven forward by the forgotten impact of past events. We act in the manner which inspired the dying Christ to say: "Father, forgive them; for they know not what they do."

The futility of such behavior lies in the fact that it never works. It fails because it attempts to redress ancient wrongs that no longer exist. Insofar as it is motivated by a fantasy, it must inevitably be aimed at the wrong target. Unconsciously, we always know that this is so—and as a result we develop a secret sense of guilt to go along with our hate. From this combination a new and vicious cycle arises. Our secret guilt makes us feel the need to punish ourselves when we hate falsely. We accomplish this by provoking counter-retaliations which bring real injury to us all over again. In that way, we not only heap the desired punishment upon ourselves but also create new justifications for our original hate.

The dreadful consequences may be seen all around us in everyday life. There is the man, for example, who maintains a perpetually hostile attitude toward his employers. He is convinced beforehand that he will always get a "raw deal," that his services and abilities will never be properly recognized. Such a man is unaware that his attitude is motivated by buried resentments whose origin perhaps goes back to real or imaginary offenses perpetrated during his childhood by unjust parents and teachers. He therefore seeks out reasons in the present to support his hostility—and since his combative attitude naturally provokes animosity where none might otherwise exist, he manages to stir up real grounds for quarrels and reprisals. He thus defeats his chances of success and may eventually end his association with a violent blowup. He now has new reasons to justify his hostility—but, in the process of gaining them, he has injured his fortunes or ruined his career entirely.

Or there is the woman who goes through life with a chronic attitude of contempt toward men. Originally her attitude may have sprung from one of several causes. She may have been disappointed in an early love affair, or it may have been that her father was a cruel and domineering man. Perhaps as a child she herself believed women to be inferior creatures, and in an effort to maintain her own self-esteem turned this feeling against men. Whatever the buried cause, her contemptuous attitude now makes it impossible for her to admit to herself that decent and considerate men exist. On the contrary, such a woman often goes out of her way to pick brutal or selfish partners as new lovers and husbands so that she may "prove" her contempt to have been justified. Her relationships then either become a living hell or end in divorce, and the woman is left to spend the rest of her years a lonely and embittered person.

Chronic hate thus compounds the evil it ostensibly sets out to redress. This is often strikingly demonstrated by the cruelties perpetrated from one generation to another. That may happen with a parent who carries into adulthood the childhood jealousies once harbored toward his little brothers and sisters. When his own children appear, such a parent uses them as mistaken substitutes for the forgotten rivals. He treats them with the excessive harshness and resentment he once had to conceal, until his children actually become delinquent offenders. The parent now has "valid" reason both to suffer from his children's misdeeds and to punish them further—and so the sorrowful cycle of hatred, revenge and self-defeat makes its full turn.

It was Edmund Burke, that wise and experienced English statesman, who exclaimed, "What shadows we are, and what shadows we pursue!" For we truly walk in shrouded ignorance when we allow our accumulated hatreds to serve as motive power for our actions. Human relationships then inevitably become a grotesque contest in which we struggle with one another not as we are, but rather like airless phantoms who can never even hear, much less understand, what one may say to the other. Chronic hate wastes our energies, sets a premium upon failures and mutual destruction. Because it blinds us to the world's real opportunities, it makes a truly successful life all but impossible.

Love's Hunger

The enigma of human relationships in everyday life remains only half solved when we have pierced the masks of hostility. For love, too, lies concealed in the secret recesses of the soul. There it stirs impatiently, like a hungry child who cannot wait to gobble up its food, and the danger is ever great that we will be driven to precipitous action not in accord with reality. In our eagerness to love, we often make the same mistake that we do with our hate. We follow ancient patterns as if they were present facts, and pour out our love for reasons that are no longer valid. Trapped into disappointment and frustration because of our misdirected emotion, we then justify our error by accusing others of betrayal or unworthiness.

Much of the bitterness that invades so many marriage relationships, for example, can be traced to this source alone. Its pattern of development is illustrated by the case of a woman who came to me for help because her marriage to a distinguished surgeon was about to collapse. She had reached the point of despair because her original expectations about the kind of life she would lead with her husband had failed to materialize. A highly educated woman, fond of art and music, she had dreamed of an active social life. She wanted to make her home a salon where leaders in art, society and politics could freely gather.

It soon became apparent, however, that her husband would never be able to share in such a life. As a successful surgeon his time and energies were completely absorbed by his work. He was on 24-hour call, and his wife could never count on his participation when she made her social plans. Their dinner parties repeatedly would be broken up because of emergency calls. Often she would have to appear alone at important events because her husband was delayed at the hospital. She began to criticize him bitterly for his lack of interest in cultural matters, and insisted that it showed a lack of true love. After several years of this kind of bickering, she felt she could no longer go on.

Exploration of the situation showed that her criticisms were entirely unfounded. The surgeon was in fact an admirable man in every respect and genuinely loved his wife. Their clash was due wholly to her false attitude, and was traced back to the love she had held for her father. He, in turn, had been a distinguished diplomat of the old school— a charming man with considerable skill as an amateur singer, a keen student of poetry and drama, and a fascinating host to visitors from all over the world. The daughter had always adored him, and when she married she transferred these earlier feelings onto her husband. She expected him to be the same kind of man her father was, and to lead the same kind of life—surrounded always by interesting people, immersed in artistic matters, eager for social adventure.

When she finally realized that her disappointments arose from her own concealed memories and expectations, her attitude changed. She was now able to see her husband in all his considerable worth. Since she had actually loved him from the start, she was able to readjust to the realities of being a surgeon's wife and to rebuild the marriage on a sound foundation.

Now it is normal to overidealize a beloved person and so make more valuable the object of our heart's desire. All lovers do this, and all marriages begin with this element present in the relationship. Yet no permanent harm results, for in true love this distortion is in time replaced by a sounder relationship based on an appreciation of the beloved's real virtues.

The damage is effected when the overidealization persists as a concealed fantasy, and can therefore never be satisfied by the reality. We then work ourselves into impossible relationships that can only lead to disaster. Such a marriage came to my notice in the case of a woman whose husband's grandiose plans had reduced her to a state of bewildered exhaustion. They had two small children. The younger suffered from heart disease and required the mother's constant care and attention. The husband nevertheless led what could only be described as a violently active life. He was a man of excessive energy and drive who always ran two or three businesses at a time, traveled incessantly, and loved to have swarms of guests constantly at his home.

When the wife came to see me she was in tears. Her husband, it appeared, had gone out West to recover from an attack of influenza, and while there he had purchased a large tract of land in a sparsely settled region remote from all centers of civilization. He now wanted the family to move to this site, which he proposed to turn into a ranch where he would breed cattle, raise chickens and go in for horticultural experiments on an elaborate scale. There was a large house on the property, and he enthusiastically pictured a gay and healthful life in which they would be able to entertain a dozen friends at a time.

It was an utterly senseless plan. In that remote region, far from available sources of labor, all the work would inevitably have devolved upon the wife. With the added burden of a sick child to attend, this could only have meant her own ultimate breakdown. But her husband could not see it in this light, and he insisted that they go forward with the plan.

He was finally prevailed upon to discuss the matter with me, and we were able to learn the reason for this stubborn attitude. His history revealed that he was one of a family of eight children. His mother, born on a European farm, was a woman of tireless energy who had been trained to run a large household with ease and efficiency. She had cooked and baked, had made the children's clothes herself, and had still found time to run a gay home that was always filled with friends and relatives. To her adoring son she was a person of omnipotent capacities, and unconsciously he had always retained this image as a picture of ideal womanhood.

It soon became clear that the son had transferred these feelings to his wife. All through their marriage he had treated her not as the person she actually was, but as a replica of his childhood image of his mother. The stubborn blindness to the realities of his marriage stemmed from the fact that emotionally he still behaved like the adoring boy who expected miracles from his mother. When he himself realized the truth, he was able to reorient his married life on a more realistic basis.

The tendency to overestimate another person's merits, so frequently a prelude to later friction in human relationships, arises from the same kind of emotional error. We have all known people who are prone to grow enthusiastic over every new friend they meet. They idealize their new acquaintances, praise them to the skies, prophesy all sorts of wonderful benefits to come from their friendship. At the same time, they begin to expect impossible services and favors as proof that their admiration was justly bestowed. Their excessive demands inevitably reach a point where they must be met with refusal. Then in a surge of disappointment, they turn their backs on their new-found friends and drop them as violently as they were at first embraced.

One must be wary of such people and not be lulled into false hopes by their initial enthusiasms. Otherwise, in business as well as in personal relationships, they may cause us great anguish and loss of both time and money. I remember a younger colleague of mine who gave up a secure professorship in a Western college, with a life tenure, to accept an offer of a more lucrative post in an Eastern college. The president of the new college was a delightful man who could sweep people off their feet with his enthusiasm and cordiality. My colleague had presented ambitious plans for the development of a new department, and these were received with great warmth, admiration, and promises of generous support.

Others warned my colleague that the new president was an unpredictable man. But my friend, caught up in the enthusiasm with which he had been welcomed, would not listen. He came East after signing a five-year contract, and at first everything went brilliantly. Then, in the middle of the second year, the picture suddenly changed without apparent cause. The president began to find fault with my colleague's work and to criticize him at every step. He became cold and aloof in their meetings, refused to co-operate in academic matters, and even withdrew funds previously promised for certain experimental projects already under way. At the end of the third year, the president notified him that his contract would not be renewed, and strongly hinted that it would be better if he found another position as soon as possible.

My colleague came to see me shortly thereafter. He was confused, angry, uncertain, and in a bitter mood as he asked my advice. "Your mistake," I told him, "was to make this president, an older man, into a sort of kind, loving father upon whom you could depend. You were unwise to have accepted a limited contract when you already had life tenure. It is true that the president was unkind and unjust in his rejection of your loyal, skillful service to the college. But you, yourself, in a sense were to blame. You should not put yourself in a position where people can take advantage of you. I am sure you will profit from this experience and not give your love and loyalty to people who cannot return it adequately."

Don't give your love to those who cannot return it! By this I do not mean that we should bring a suspicious attitude to our relationships with other people. I refer rather to the common error made when we assume that other people will love us merely because we love them. This is a false expectation based on a childish wish; it ignores the fact that others may have perfectly valid reasons to direct their love energies elsewhere. We must learn to accept this truth if we would spare ourselves the painful disillusions that not only embitter life, but also destroy our confidence in our own abilities and achievements.

It is one thing to have faith, and to hold great men in mind as ideal figures whom we can admire and emulate. That is a normal development of the child's attitude of trust and admiration toward his parents. It is the basis of the beneficial influence exerted by great teachers and statesmen. Without it, we would have no civilization, no faith in a Divine Being, no standard of achievement at which to aim It is the force that unites men under a common goal and that creates the stabilizing morale in all organizations —whether business, church or army. Love and loyalty toward a leader is the very substance on which society thrives. It was this attitude toward Robert E. Lee which held a ragged and dwindling army of Confederate soldiers together to the last despairing days of Appomattox. The healing art of the physician is itself based on such confidence and faith, and many miraculous cures spring wholly from it.

But it is another thing to endow people with qualities and virtues they do not possess. Love given on such a basis creates only havoc and folly in everyday relationships. It perpetuates infantile patterns of self-delusion and unfits us for effective dealing with our fellow men. To hitch one's wagon to a star is a noble course in life—but we must always make sure it *is* a star. One way we can do this is to make no basic assumptions about others until we have had a chance to see them in action. The mature person maintains a friendly and open-minded attitude toward all: like the scientist, he is willing to wait for concrete evidence before he arrives at a final judgment. When our love is so based, we stand on solid ground and cannot easily be shaken from our purpose.

The Touchstone of Reality

One might summarize the common errors made in everyday relationships with the statement that we all suffer from an embarrassment of emotional riches. With few exceptions, we all create an overflow of both love and hate within our hearts, and are then faced with the need to dispose of our emotions whether or not a suitable channel of expression lies at hand. Our mistakes are not due simply to love or hate in themselves. We commit errors because, under the urgent pressure of these accumulated emotional forces, *we are driven to love or hate the wrong people, at the wrong time, for the wrong reasons.*

A major task in life must therefore be a constant self-examination that will teach us to guide these errant forces to their proper goals. We must learn to hold our emotions in abeyance until we have absorbed the *facts* and *realities* of a given situation. Just as a successful financier does not invest his money until he investigates the real conditions of the market, so a wise man does not formulate emotional reactions until he has determined whether they are justified by the actual circumstances present in his relationships with other people.

When troublesome conflicts and disturbances arise, the

167

wise man automatically meets the problem with a series of questions directed to himself. He asks: "Is there a preconceived emotional attitude behind these actions? Am I viewing the situation with a secret hate or a false love that I have carried over from the past? Is the other fellow's behavior similarly motivated? Is he using the present disturbance as an excuse to work off buried emotions whose existence he himself does not suspect?"

He then proceeds to take steps *based on the reality of the situation,* rather than on its false emotional background. The elder J. P. Morgan once shrewdly declared: "A man always has two reasons for doing anything—a good reason and the real reason." In dealing with people, we must bear this constantly in mind. Otherwise we may be trapped by their emotional errors into taking measures that have nothing to do with the real issue involved. We may be led to rely on their judgments and opinions, when actually their own emotional "displacements" may cast a wholly distorted shadow upon the true facts.

Administrators and executives, for example, are constantly faced with this danger when they are called upon to adjust the problems that arise among their staffs. The average business office is often a hotbed of intrigues, resentments and rivalries based on concealed emotional attitudes rather than on actual facts. One member of a staff, because he has never left behind the resentment once entertained toward an elder and stronger brother, may use his best energies in schemes designed to oust other members who appear to be more securely entrenched in the organization than himself. Another member may never have gotten over

The Impatient Heart

the sense of abuse developed because as a child he was given less favored treatment than other children in the family. Such a person will constantly come up with gripes and demands that can be satisfied only at the cost of ill will among the rest. The executive must see through these disguises of hostility and refuse to participate in the masquerade. Otherwise, his organization will deteriorate into a brawling nursery where all the members use the best part of their working energies simply to frustrate one another.

The touchstone of reality must automatically be applied whenever one's behavior is characterized by overintense emotions either of love or of hate. When a conflict or a state of resentment persists beyond a reasonable time, we may safely suspect that preconceived attitudes and concealed emotions are the underlying cause. At such times, all attempts to deal with the issues at their face value will be doomed to failure. That is why labor disputes, for example, so often reach an impasse marked by blind stubbornness and violent animosity. The quarrel ostensibly is over wages and hours, when actually it is an emotional battle in which the workers play the role of resentful children and the employers are the tyrannical parents.

The course of reality in such situations is to admit to ourselves the existence of these secret motives for our behavior. Often this in itself serves as the lightning stroke that clears the clouded emotional atmosphere. We are then able to recognize where our energies have been wasted in false directions, and even to smile with relief at the revelation of our own self-deceptions. Once we have reached that point, we are in a position to examine the facts with calm objectivity. In many instances it will turn out that no real basis for conflict exists. Where a genuine difference remains, it becomes relatively easy to hurdle the impasse with an effective settlement that does justice to both sides.

Our happiness rests on our willingness to strive for this kind of realistic action. Success or failure in life depends on the nature of the emotional relationships we make with other people. The life lines that keep us all afloat are the ties of genuine love we are able to maintain despite the many destructive forces that eat at their strands. When we act toward others on the basis of our own preconceived emotional attitudes, the way is open for these insidious elements to attack us at their corrosive worst. Our armor against this danger is a firm adherence to objective truth—for that is the only pathway along which mutual love can flourish.

CHAPTER NINE

The Middle Years and Beyond

IT IS a familiar trait of human nature that men cling as long as possible to the delusion of their own indestructibility. In youth none of us believes we shall ever grow old, and to the very end our unconscious mind cannot conceive of our own death. Yet there is a point midway in life when physiological changes compel us at last to admit to ourselves that we, too, must succumb to time's inexorable toll. The realization comes as a profound shock and often precipitates a period of intense anxiety. Unless we have learned to meet life with a loving heart, we may be overwhelmed at this juncture by a morbid depression, the effects of which will remain ever after to cripple us in both body and spirit.

Everyone may expect to undergo a certain amount of apprehension during the transitional crisis of these middle years. It is perfectly normal to react with dismay at the appearance of our first gray hairs, or to grow alarmed when

171

suddenly the printed page blurs before our eyes. Any change in one's accustomed adjustment to the environment always arouses primitive fears for our safety, and it is natural enough that we should experience qualms when visible signs give proof that youth's full powers are no longer at our command. Such fears serve a valuable purpose if they lead us to readapt our way of life and to take practical measures as a safeguard against the future.

The unhappiness so often found in middle age does not lie in the changes it brings, but in our refusal to accept them as a normal part of nature's flowing design. At other transitional periods of life, we do not question the need for making the proper readjustments—although the bridge from childhood to adolescence, or from adolescence to maturity, may be inherently even more difficult to traverse. When we reach the middle years, however, men and women are likely to be thrown into a state of panic which prevents them from taking a balanced view of their problem. They distort it beyond its true proportions, and seek strenuously either to deny or to exaggerate the physiological changes that occur at this time.

Some react with frantic efforts to prove they are better than ever before. Men and women in their forties proverbially try to maintain an artificial, glassy kind of youthfulness that deceives no one but themselves. They become overvivacious and dashing, and exhaust themselves in a dizzy round of social activities. In the business world, we often see a counterpart in those anxious, fear-ridden men who redouble their hours of work as a smokescreen to throw around their age. They devote themselves completely

172

The Middle Years and Beyond

to their job, take few or no holidays, and even find excuses to go down to the office on Sundays. Such persons behave as if, like Joshua, they could command the sun and moon to stand still in their flight across the heavens. Actually, they either fall victim to obesity and high blood pressure, or they grow thin and nervous and suffer from insomnia. In the end, they often have a nervous breakdown from which they may never fully recover.

Other men and women go to the opposite extreme and conclude bitterly that life is as good as over for them. They fall back on an attitude of grim disillusion about the world, are apt to become morbidly concerned about every detail of their health, and do little to free their remaining years from the loneliness and futility which inevitably overtake them. Men are likely to develop this pattern of reaction when their careers have failed to keep pace with the ambitions of their youth; women, after their children grow up and leave home. They are left with the feeling that they are worn out and useless, and are convinced they can never again play an important role in life. The attack of anxiety or depression may be further accentuated by the death of one's own parents, which often occurs around this period and may revive earlier emotions of helplessness or desertion.

Now the close of youth is a logical point for re-evaluation of one's past achievements and future goals. Often it brings waves of sorrow for follies unnecessarily committed, as well as pangs of regret for hopes that never materialized. "The life of every man," as J. M. Barrie put it, "is a diary in which he means to write one story, and writes another; and his humblest hour is when he compares the volume as

173

Love or Perish

it is with what he vowed to make it." But moments of self-appraisal like these help place one's course of life in better perspective. Without them, we might not be able to reset our sights on realistic objectives instead of unattainable dreams.

It is an altogether different matter when we turn self-appraisal into self-laceration and use it as proof that our lives are doomed. I once had occasion to observe the tragic consequences of such an attitude in the case of a man who otherwise had every reason to look forward with confidence to the future. He was a successful stockbroker, the owner of his own business at 45, and one of those perennial undergraduates who derive their greatest pleasures from active participation with fellow alumni in college affairs.

The critical point in his life came at a week-end reunion with a group of classmates. There was the usual vigorous round of celebration, and on the last day he played three sets of tennis under a broiling sun. Physical activity had never before caused him undue strain; but this time he collapsed in utter exhaustion at the end of the match. His heart pounded furiously in his chest as he lay stretched out on a bench, his breath came in convulsive gasps for half an hour, and it took him several days before he was able to get over the debilitating effects.

A marked change came over the man soon afterward. Despite his physician's assurance that he had merely over-exerted himself and would simply have to be more careful in the future, he became convinced that he had suffered a serious heart attack. He grew morose and brooded secretly over what he felt certain was an imminent collapse. He be-

174

gan to buttonhole acquaintances and complain about his wasted life, although he insisted in the same breath that it was too late to change.

By the time he was fifty he had become a confirmed hypochondriac—fearful, suspicious, pessimistic. He spent his birthday moaning aloud to his family and friends: "I'm through. . . . It's no use—life's over for me!" All during this period he was actually in good physical health; and it wasn't until a year later that he had to go to the hospital for a minor operation to remove a small cyst on his back. He was ready to return home, fully recovered, when on the last day in the hospital he suddenly contracted pneumonia. Despite all measures, he sank steadily and died a few days later.

Those who knew him intimately realized that he was a man who had lost the will to live. He was unable to accept the fact that one cannot remain a youthful undergraduate forever. The revelation of a flaw in his physical powers had left him morbidly ashamed; and he feared he could no longer compete successfully with other men. Like many who see the world chiefly in terms of aggression and conquest, he could not conceive of any modification in his way of life which would bring satisfaction and happiness. The crisis of middle age, in other words, had found him psychologically defenseless when it threatened to deplete the raw youthful energy that had been his only form of strength.

Fortunately, most of us possess sufficient reserve powers to pull through such crises. We do not lose our grip on life entirely—yet we all stand exposed in some degree to the same danger of being trapped without adequate psychological defenses at a moment when we need them most acutely. In earlier years we may rely on sheer abundance of energy to offset the toll claimed by inner anxieties, concealed resentments, suppressed guilts. But we cannot blanket this buried time bomb of emotion indefinitely. Our powers of resistance diminish after forty; and if we have not already learned how to turn our psychic forces to constructive use, the pressure mounts and an explosion must occur. In psychiatric terms, our unconscious fears and resentments will then rise so close to the surface of the conscious mind that we will no longer be able to deflect their devastating impact.

Our choice at this point is clear-cut. If we have based our past life on neurotic lies, we must now abandon them once and for all—or we will surely be crushed by the accumulated weight of our own errors and self-deceptions. It was Swift who declared: "The latter part of a wise man's life is taken up in curing the follies, prejudices and false opinions he has contracted in the former." Unless we equip ourselves to do this, we cannot expect to deal effectively with the special hazards of the later years.

Our Secret Specter

The crucial aspect of middle age lies in the fact that it brings an unusually severe test of our ability to use love as the guiding force in life. Love speaks in a thousand tongues, some of which we understand automatically at birth. Up to a certain point, we can get along well enough with this limited knowledge of its speech. But as life moves past its zenith, we are confronted with a special problem that will leave us hopelessly baffled unless we develop great skill in the use of love's infinite language.

In youth we are protected by a blind power of love which nature gives indiscriminately to all of us. The basic purpose of life, in the biological sense, is to create and preserve new life. Whatever else we may do, however grossly we may distort or violate the proper unfoldment of our life's design, we at least serve love's imperious command when we re-produce and rear a new creature to take our place after we are gone. It is because we are all driven despite ourselves to fulfill this eternal goal that the human race has managed to survive its own endless follies.

Unconsciously, we all draw impregnable strength from our knowledge that this is so. It is immaterial to our sense of omnipotence whether we carry out the task poorly or well—or, indeed, whether or not we subsequently mar our handiwork through perversity and destructiveness. We de-velop the illusion of limitless resources at our disposal, and we are sublimely careless of all waste or error. As long as we possess the power to re-create life, we feel sure that love is on our side and no serious harm can befall us.

The one great catastrophe we all unconsciously fear is that we will lose or be deprived of this basic, primitive power. In youth we are not as a rule seriously disturbed by such fears, although they play a role in normal character de-velopment and may become accentuated enough to con-tribute toward a neurosis. But as we grow older, what was once considered to be a remote possibility suddenly looms up as a distinct reality. However incredible it may seem, there comes a time when we are brought face to face with the disaster we dreaded most of all—a decline in our physical powers, and with it the threat of a loss in sexual potency.

Few of us can brave this critical development with unflinching courage. For, in the unconscious, it is always interpreted as a threat against life itself! We may try to convince ourselves that it is simply a normal physiological change; and consciously we may bolster our faint hearts with statistical proof of useful decades yet to come. But in the deeper levels of the mind we view it as an assault upon the one great power which has always given us our sense of immortality. We feel we have lost our partnership with love; hence, also, our blind assurance of eternal victory. Stripped of this protection, we imagine ourselves left like helpless or mutilated children who no longer possess the magic armor that will ward off the mortal blows of fate.

Here is the special problem, the central anxiety behind the crisis of middle age. We may advance other plausible reasons to justify our panic: traditionally, one cites the danger of falling victim to illness, neglect, loneliness and all the other handicaps that may afflict us in later years. True, these are formidable hazards and may one day become real problems for us to solve. But at this point we use them merely as pretexts. At bottom, the secret specter which haunts our souls so darkly is rather the fear that we will be left without the power to re-create life. And in our unconscious minds, this deprivation takes on an added significance. It becomes, psychologically, the equivalent of losing life itself.

If we have not learned the deeper and fuller meaning of love, we may now be at a loss for an effective solution to the problem before us. The characteristic disturbances of later life often arise because, in our bewilderment, we are driven to false paths of behavior whose main purpose is rather to avoid or to conceal the problem altogether. One recognizes the escape aspect easily when we come upon the middle-aged Lothario with his chorus girl, or the dancing grandmother with her gigolo. But there are widespread behavior patterns in subtler and more disguised form which have the same motivation. They cause infinitely more harm because we usually fail to understand their true origin.

It is typical of many men and women past fifty, for example, to develop a distorted attitude toward money. They begin either to spend it so foolishly, or to make such a fetish of saving it, that they actually bring suffering to those dependent upon them. Men often couple this with a morbid fear that their business is going to fail. Although they derive a perfectly adequate income from their work, they hoard their assets to an extent that deprives their families of all but the fundamental necessities of life. In their business they talk of nothing but hard times. They will postpone payment of bills to the point where they seriously damage their credit standing; and often their unjustified economies lead to bankruptcy. Men of this type are usually very nervous, suffer from insomnia, or cannot remain still for five minutes at a time. They make life quite miserable for their families and are avoided by their former friends. Rarely do they escape without a major physical breakdown.

This abnormal pattern of behavior, centered as it is around a morbid concern about money, is a fictitious method of preserving one's physical and sexual powers. Money, of course, is a symbol of all that is valuable in life; over and above its actual worth, we ascribe to it a magical power that can command the gratification of every wish. That is why men and women universally use it as a sub-stitute for whatever else they may lack in life.

The niggardliness so often encountered among wealthy older people is a glaring example of financial power used to compensate for waning physical and sexual power. It can spread a great deal of unhappiness in life. One of my patients, a young woman preparing for a professional career, endured serious hardships because her divorced parents (both millionaires) refused to give her any financial help. The mother went to incredible lengths to assert her superior power over the young woman. She would go so far as to demand payment in cash every time her daughter, while visiting her, made a telephone call.

In another case that came to my attention, a young man almost had to abandon his medical career because of his father's distorted attitude toward money. He wanted to specialize in surgery, which would require several years of additional training beyond medical school. But his father, although a man of wealth, took refuge behind the common belief that one only "pauperizes" people by helping them out. "You will have to make your own way," he told his son. The boy managed to continue his studies, but only at the cost of extreme privations. He never got over his bitterness toward his father, and broke off all relations with him. The older man's false expression of power thus denied to himself the happiness he might have had later from the love of his son and grandchildren.

Illness is another widely adopted form of compensation, especially among women. All intelligent physicians know that at least half their middle-aged patients come to them mainly for reassurance or attention. A standard type of medical patient is the woman who runs from doctor to doctor in the hope that at least one of them will take a serious view of her minor symptoms. Such women use their ailments as a distorted substitute for their fading powers of attraction. They are particularly fond of operations: surgery is a dramatic episode in which they again take the center of the stage as the young heroine in distress. They are rescued by the surgeon in the role of gallant champion, and for a long time afterward remain the object of universal solicitude among family and friends.

A less specific but equally barren substitute is the chronic pessimism developed by so many men and women in later life. They view the world with anxiety and alarm, and take every opportunity to insist that it is going to the dogs. Such people merely project their personal feelings of inadequacy onto external events. I knew one woman in her early forties, for example, who always greeted her friends with some such exclamation as: "Isn't it awful what is happening in Europe!" or perhaps: "Did you read that terrible story in the papers this morning!" She was a successful interior decorator and an attractive woman; but she had been twice divorced and obviously had little hope left of achieving a happy marital relationship. She might still have done so had she come to grips with her own inner problem. Instead, she worried constantly about such things as social injustice and economic exploitation, but took no action, and was always in a turmoil about one public cause or another.

Older people often express their sense of personal inadequacy through condemnation of the younger generation— whether for its lack of morals, or thrift, or devotion to duty. Failing that, the political situation is a favorite source of concern. Many years ago I met a 74-year-old man who was in constant fear that the government of the United States would go bankrupt. He was worth more than a million dollars, and after the stock market crash of 1929 had invested most of this in government bonds. "Don't you know," he insisted, "that the bottom would drop out if the government did not artificially support the bonds?" I tried to reassure him that in any event he would salvage enough to provide for his remaining years. He only shook his head and replied: "The world is in a bad state—it's a very depressing situation!"

Mental attitudes and behavior patterns like these cause a vast amount of misery in the world. Individuals so afflicted dissipate most of their energies in sterile pursuits, spend a good portion of their lives under a pall of gloom. Even worse, they inflict untold injury upon those associated with them. The chronically ill woman, for example, often imposes severe emotional and financial burdens upon her family. One of the more sorrowful aspects is that younger lives may be permanently warped as a consequence.

The Middle Years and Beyond

Yet much of this appalling waste can be avoided if we seize the gift of love properly and shape it to our human purposes. Too many of us assume that love will be automatically denied to us as we enter upon the later years. This is a fallacy we must learn to correct.

The Scale of Love

In the realm of nature, love follows a rising scale of complexity. It is relatively simple on the lowest level of organic life, where it is concerned solely with a single cell. There it provides the cell with the balance necessary to maintain itself and to reproduce through subdivision—a cycle which takes less than an hour to complete.

As the structure of living organisms becomes more complex, so does the task of love. It must now hold many cells together; and it must also bring about a union of different cells before reproduction can take place. The task then grows ever more involved and lengthy the higher we go in the animal scale. Among the more primitive species, the offspring are still abandoned to their own devices immediately after birth. But the higher mammals continue with love's nurture long beyond this point—until, among humans, the care and preservation of the young becomes one of the major activities of mankind. Instead of being limited simply to the biological cycle of reproduction, it expands into a virtually lifelong process.

The truth is that love, in all its creative and nurturing forms of expression, spreads out through the web of human life to an extent elsewhere unparalleled. Its ramifications are so infinite in number that we may justly consider this to be the chief mark of distinction between mankind and all other forms of life on earth.

One may go even further and say that almost everything specifically human—as contrasted with the rest of the animal world—is a product of love. For man alone among all living creatures perpetuates his own kind through his ability to control and modify the external forces of nature. His specific *humanity,* that is, consists of three basic arts peculiar to him alone. Man has developed the art of agriculture, whereby he manipulates the forces of nature to provide his supply of food at will; he has perfected the art of making fire and tools, whereby he creates his own means of shelter and protection; and, finally, he has evolved the art of speech and writing, which gives him the means of education whereby all the other arts may be communicated and preserved from one generation to another. Each of these arts is inspired by human love and is an expression of it, for their goal is to help create and preserve new life in its human form.

On this basis, we may formulate the fundamental law which all of us must obey. Whereas other living organisms will perish if they do not adapt *themselves* to the environment, man must also change the *environment* in order to preserve himself as a human being. But he can do so only if he uses the arts of love in the human sense. It is therefore correct to say: *Man must love or perish!*

The great error all of us are likely to make in middle age is to forget this human law, and to revert to the conception of love in its primitive biological form alone! There is a reason for this. It is almost as if the change of life in men and women unconsciously compels us to recollect an earlier stage of evolution when—as in the dayfly or the salmon—the parent organism dies soon after its mission of reproduction has been fulfilled. We naturally become depressed at this time, for the biological change we undergo revives the sense that love has been taken from our lives altogether. Yet we may successfully move to combat our depression as a passing phase if we will remember two basic truths.

The first truth is this: Human life is *not* carried out solely on a primitive biological level. At the human stage of evolution, we do *not* die upon reaching the middle phase of life. Certain limitations develop, of course, and must be accepted. We are never again as powerful physically as we are in our twenties; at fifty, we can no longer play football or dance the whole night through. But the fact is that we normally retain sufficient virility and strength to serve us more than amply for two or three decades to come. Few of us are ever so enfeebled that we cannot pursue a normal life.

The second truth to remember is this: Our opportunities for the expression of love in its characteristically human aspects may actually increase as we grow older. If we have learned the lesson that love's task merely *begins* with the biological creation of new life, we can use our years of knowledge and skill to carry it out in a broader and richer manner than ever before. We will be conscious of the fact that in human life there is no end to the need for the arts of love, which offer innumerable channels of activity. Men and women can create, invent, produce, nurture and educate until their very last days on earth!

Statistics show, in fact, that they do these things better in the latter part of life. The American sociologist, W. A. M. Dorland, some years ago published the results of his research into the age at which men and women produce their most important works. He included such varied groups as chemists, writers, explorers, mathematicians, naturalists and jurists. All of these did their best work between the ages of 40 and 60! The chemists were at the younger end of the list, with the average at 41 for their best achievements. Jurists and naturalists were at the older end of the table, with 59 their average peak age.

It is highly significant that men who devote their lives exclusively to these arts of love often work actively to a very advanced age, even when handicapped by severe infirmities. The great Italian painter, Titian, lived to the age of 99 and continued work practically until his final year. The great French biologist, Lamarck, dictated his *Histoire Naturelle* until his death at the age of 85. Alexander von Humboldt, the great German scientist and philosopher, began writing his *Kosmos* at the age of 74 and worked on it until his death at the age of 90. Dr. Benjamin M. Duggar discovered the "wonder drug" aureomycin when he was 71 years old, after his compulsory retirement from the University of Wisconsin. Milton dictated his last poems to his daughters even though he was then completely blind; and Beethoven composed his last great symphonies and quartets when he was totally deaf. Sigmund Freud was stricken with cancer of his upper jaw and underwent twenty-five operations for it. He was in constant pain, yet he continued to work until his death fifteen years later.

Another remarkable example of what love can do for the human spirit was afforded by the French painter, Renoir. That modern master worked joyously at his beloved easel even though he was so crippled by rheumatism during his last two decades that he had to be carried everywhere in a chair and could not hold the paint brushes in his fingers. He would have the brushes tied to his wrist, and in this manner produced some of his most beautiful work in the years before his death at the age of 78. The power of love to triumph over all adversity perhaps never received a more awe-inspiring expression than when this heroic old man remarked to his friends that he had no right to complain, since "things might have been worse."

One may object that these were exceptional men in the history of mankind, and not everyone can hope to possess such extraordinary powers. True, their work was exceptional—but the spirit of creative love which animated their lives is something all may achieve. I have seen innumerable instances, in every walk of life, where men and women maintained a courageous and constructive attitude despite all the setbacks of their later years. I knew a nurse, for example, who was stricken at the age of 50 with an incurable disease that left her partially paralyzed. She knew she had only a few remaining years, at best, ahead of her. Nevertheless, her life had been so completely centered on the task of caring for other people that she simply could not give up. She continued to work part time at her hospital as long as she was able to hobble about, and her example of cheerfulness and courage served as an inspiration to all the patients around her.

In several cases, I have seen women take up new professions at a time of life when many of us feel our work is almost over. One of these was a housewife whose husband died suddenly when she was about 45 years old. She had by then raised a family of four children, but she refused to depend on them as an emotional outlet. Instead she decided to carry on the work of her husband, who had conducted experimental farming for the Department of Agriculture. She went to school, took special courses, and at the age of 70 is still busy in her new career—a happy and contented woman.

Another woman of 65 found a similar solution to her problem of loneliness after her husband died. Although she never could have children of her own, she had always had a special fondness and sympathy for youngsters in their teens. Now, oppressed with the monotony of her life, she resolved to go to school and perfect herself in the art of cooking, for which she had always had a natural gift. She then took a large apartment near one of the city universities where students were in need of living quarters. She found six girls to move in with her, and created for them a lovely home where she acted as housekeeper and mother. Youngsters often find that women of this type have a better insight into their problems than their own mothers. In this instance, the woman built up warm relationships with all of the girls, and she has continued her new activity happily for more than ten years.

The Middle Years and Beyond

Men have a special problem when compulsory retirement leaves them without an activity in life. I strongly believe that a man should never retire as long as he is able to do useful work. Modern industrial society does not take this problem sufficiently into account, and often it is difficult for the individual to solve it by himself. Nevertheless there are ways of doing it, provided we retain a constructive and outgoing attitude. Some years ago I was consulted by a widower of 68 who had worked most of his life as a supervisor in the car shops of a railroad. He had been retired on a small pension that provided him with the bare necessities of life. He was quite lonely and unhappy because of his enforced idleness, yet felt it would be unwise to foist himself upon either of his two married children.

Our discussion revealed that he had always been fond of golf, and had once toyed with the idea of starting a driving range on his own. Since one of his sons lived near a Southern resort town, I suggested he go there and investigate the possibilities of carrying out his earlier plan. He leaped at the idea, and before long had carried it out in a simple way by opening a small driving range. There he met a businessman who agreed to finance his plans for further expansion. The business grew and became a source of both pleasure and profit for him. Today, instead of being a depressed and lonely old man of 73, he is vigorous, cheerful and optimistic about the future and, incidentally, plays a good game of golf.

"People always say your days are numbered when you grow old," he remarked to me when I saw him not long ago. Then he smiled as he added, "You know what—your days are numbered from the time you are born! I get more pleasure out of life than I ever did before, and I look forward to many years of happy work!"

Not all persons in their sixties, of course, possess the special kind of enterprise required to start a new business. But there are more solutions to the practical problems of life than we ordinarily suspect. It is the *depression* felt about growing old that makes things seem so hopeless, rather than old age itself. Conquer this, and half the practical problems disappear.

I knew a professor of biology who learned at the age of 67 that he was seriously ill with an abdominal cancer. He had passed the compulsory retirement age of his college, and he was alone in the world: his only child, a son, had been killed in the last war, and his wife had died two years before. His physicians advised that an operation be performed—and, at that point, one might have forgiven him had he lost the will to live any further. Yet he felt he had a continuing obligation to transmit his store of specialized knowledge to younger generations of students. It had taken him years to acquire it, and he considered it a duty to perpetuate his scientific heritage as long as he could. He recovered from the operation, and soon obtained a post on a university faculty that had been especially established for retired professors. This man is now 82 years of age, and is still teaching successfully.

The truth is that the world is desperately in need of the knowledge, wisdom and skill older people are in so favorable a position to supply. In his *The Shape of Things to Come,* H. G. Wells observed: "The years from 30 to 70

The Middle Years and Beyond

were formerly a sort of dump for the consequences of the first three decades; now they are the main part of life, the years of work, expression and complete self-discovery, to which these earlier stages are the bright, delightful prelude." Not all may agree—for the temper of our times, at least in American society, seems to be hostile toward old age. Our pioneer heritage has emphasized the cult of youthfulness at all costs, and we do not particularly esteem the "wise old men" in our midst.

Such an attitude is justified insofar as it is applied to older men and women who sit back and expect the world to beat a path of homage to their door. Many older people make that mistake. They regress to an earlier period of life and act like children who demand love constantly, but give none back. It is important to remember that true love consists of giving to others as well as getting; and this remains so to the last. Older people may insist that they have earned love as a reward for past deeds. But others rarely acknowledge the debt even if it exists, and we doom ourselves to bitterness and neglect if we expect automatic payment.

Both society and the individual must learn to take the better alternative that is available. The true wisdom of age is a precious ingredient we can ill afford to waste. All of us have it within our power to acquire at least some portion of that ingredient, provided we retain our attitude of love toward the world. Then we will possess a commodity that society will value. Then, too, each of us will possess the magic device that can make the later years of life an era of new growth and fulfillment.

Lovability

Amid the

the twentieth century," in Winston Ch

any plea for greater love in human affa

naïve and old-fashioned. For modern

tough and "practical" in its approach t

part sees little reason to concern itsel

emotional needs. Its psychological stru

material concept of human welfare, and

largely by the tangible assets one can pro

in the market place of the external w

problems of love and hate have smal

trade, they are either relegated to the

romance or else regarded as a nuisanc

solve in private as best one can.

Yet, for all our outward toughness,

very deep to discover the aching emo

Our need for love, as I have tried to sh

The Middle Years and Beyond

were formerly a sort of dump for the consequences of the first three decades; now they are the main part of life, the years of work, expression and complete self-discovery, to which these earlier stages are the bright, delightful prelude." Not all may agree—for the temper of our times, at least in American society, seems to be hostile toward old age. Our pioneer heritage has emphasized the cult of youthfulness at all costs, and we do not particularly esteem the "wise old men" in our midst.

Such an attitude is justified insofar as it is applied to older men and women who sit back and expect the world to beat a path of homage to their door. Many older people make that mistake. They regress to an earlier period of life and act like children who demand love constantly, but give none back. It is important to remember that true love consists of giving to others as well as getting; and this remains so to the last. Older people may insist that they have earned love as a reward for past deeds. But others rarely acknowledge the debt even if it exists, and we doom ourselves to bitterness and neglect if we expect automatic payment.

Both society and the individual must learn to take the better alternative that is available. The true wisdom of age is a precious ingredient we can ill afford to waste. All of us have it within our power to acquire at least some portion of that ingredient, provided we retain our attitude of love toward the world. Then we will possess a commodity that society will value. Then, too, each of us will possess the magic device that can make the later years of life an era of new growth and fulfillment.

CHAPTER TEN

Lovability

Amid the "lusty squalor of the twentieth century," in Winston Churchill's apt phrase, any plea for greater love in human affairs may well sound naïve and old-fashioned. For modern industrial society, tough and "practical" in its approach to life, for the most part sees little reason to concern itself with man's inner emotional needs. Its psychological structure is based on a material concept of human welfare, and it measures success largely by the tangible assets one can produce and exchange in the market place of the external world. Since human problems of love and hate have small value as items of trade, they are either relegated to the realm of fictional romance or else regarded as a nuisance that one must resolve in private as best one can.

Yet, for all our outward toughness, one need not probe very deep to discover the aching emotional void beneath. Our need for love, as I have tried to show in the preceding

Lovability

chapters of this book, is a basic reality whose power to shape the course of life is greater than that of any material force in the world outside. Men may present a brave front with the hard-boiled philosophy of our times, but they cannot conceal the emotional breakdowns which bring one out of every twelve persons in this country to a mental institution for treatment at some point of their lives. We may officially extol the virtues of our fiercely competitive scramble for the material prizes of the world, but it needs only casual observation to tell us that in private we suffer almost universally from a profound undercurrent of loneliness, depression and insecurity.

If we wish to bring more love into our lives, therefore, we must begin by taking a simple first step. We must acknowledge openly—both to ourselves and to one another—that we all do in truth need and want love. We must state this fact in no uncertain terms and boldly declare it to be our conviction that the world can no longer afford to ignore its significance. As a further step, we must vigorously reaffirm our belief that the gratification of these emotional needs is not only a valid goal for mature men to pursue, but is also an indispensable requisite of human happiness without which life can have no true meaning.

Too many of us have maintained silence on this score as we have watched man rush onward for more than a century in his insatiable desire to conquer nature. Intimidated by the brilliance of modern inventive genius, we have permitted one scientific miracle after another to be substituted for the infinitely greater wonders of the human heart. Our increasing reliance on staggeringly complex mechanical in-

193

struments has subtly shaken our self-esteem to a point where man is no longer certain of his own individual worth. By our acquiescence in this tacit contempt for human beings, we have imperiled the stability of society and, in the midst of material abundance, reaped an emotional harvest of disillusion, frustration and anxiety.

Not long ago I witnessed an instance of this psychological distress as it developed among people I knew in a small town. They were a group of telephone operators whose long service had built up an affectionate personal relationship with almost everyone in the community. But one fateful day the automatic dial system was installed, and with it their entire lives were undermined at a stroke.

No economic hardship was involved, for they were all shifted to other jobs elsewhere at the same salaries. It was the blow to their pride—to their sense of usefulness and importance as human beings—which darkened their spirit. For example, many of the subscribers were their friends and they enjoyed a cheery good morning, or a sympathetic grousing about the weather. They felt humiliated at being replaced by an electronic device (however more efficient) and were deeply saddened by the loss of the warm, human contacts they had valued for so many years. They had no choice, however, but to accept the inevitable march of "progress" in silence, and to hide their unhappiness as best they could.

Our first step, I repeat, must be to break this silence. I believe that mankind, secretly starved for lack of love, yearns desperately to have its plight recognized and its emotional claims supported. Men and women are not content

Lovability

to hear their inner aspirations voiced merely in the maudlin accents of mass-entertainment media, for these offer only fantasies which do nothing to alter the essential burden of their lives. They wish to have their needs fulfilled in the world of action—in business, in politics, in everyday human contact. Yet our prevailing social philosophy places a premium upon the suppression of our craving for warm human relations, and ordinarily one does not dare give expression to it for fear of general ridicule.

We are all oppressed, far more than we realize, by this enforced concealment of our hopes and desires. Its unspoken betrayal of human integrity evokes deep resentments that emerge to plague us in disguised forms, of which the brutal cynicism so often encountered in modern life is but one example.

An open avowal of the need for love in every aspect of life can therefore serve as an emotional release and a rallying point for a new approach to our personal, social and economic problems. It will enable us to focus our attention on the real source of disturbance in contemporary life—which is the collective pressure constantly exerted upon us to use our aggressive drives at the expense of our love impulses.

As long as we remain inarticulate in our opposition to this trend, we can do little to resist the flood of purely destructive emotion it sets loose. We must make a clear statement of our determination to restore the balance of forces, and thus to regain proper control of our basic energies, if we wish to move forward on the road that will bring more love into our individual lives.

Love or Perish

Our Urge Toward Goodness

Now, it is obvious that every normal person must approach life with a practical concern for his economic welfare. We depend on the material world for the gratification of basic physical needs, and no one familiar with the blight spread by poverty and deprivation would deny that man's economic well-being is a vital factor in human happiness. One may even say that in a free society an individual's failure to meet this essential requirement is itself often a sign of psychological maladjustment.

Yet there is another kind of well-being which is of far greater importance for man's true happiness. It comes when we have satisfied the compelling need in every human being to prove to the outside world that he is a "good" person, and hence someone worthy of being loved. The urge to do so is rooted deep in our natures. It first arises when we are called upon as infants to give such proof to our parents. Because this behavior pattern enables us to win the love and protection we need for our very survival, it remains engraved in the unconscious mind as the primary means whereby one obtains the most precious things of life. That is why material possessions in themselves can never bring us full satisfaction or serve to quiet our inner anxieties. Our concept of blissful fulfillment is eternally based on the memory of the original mother-child relationship, and we feel emotionally secure only when we again win the approval and love of others as reward for our own individual, human goodness.

196

Lovability

To be a lovable person in the deepest sense, therefore, it follows that we must re-create an adult version of the good qualities originally evolved in the relationship between mother and child.

What, specifically, are these qualities? The answer is contained in the twofold, reciprocal nature of the early infantile situation. On the one hand, the mother is good and lovable primarily because she is the giver of life, the source of nourishment that sustains it, and (with the father) the guardian against all harm. She is generous, patient and forgiving. Her strength and devotion—again, with the father's—give us confidence and courage. She is lovable, that is, because she is profoundly concerned with our own welfare and provides us with all that is good in the world.

The child, on the other hand, becomes lovable and worthy of these gifts only if he learns to curb the hostile emotions that inevitably arise toward the parent. As we have seen, the infant reacts with rage when his demands are not instantly met. He hates his mother when she opposes his desires in any way, and his primitive response at such times is to wish for her destruction. But in the normal course of development the child discovers that he cannot preserve her goodness unless he controls his impulses of aggression toward her. Instead of going into tantrums when he is thwarted, he learns to accept delays in the gratification of his wishes. He abandons his imperious attitude toward the world and learns not to make impossible demands. Gradually he realizes that he must offer love to his parents in return for theirs. In substance, a "good" child is one who *gives up hate as a means of getting what he wants in life.*

Love or Perish

The secret of true lovability lies in the combined virtues derived from this reciprocal pattern of exchange. All of us retain a childlike core in our natures, and in our dealings with other people throughout life we constantly search for substitutes to replace the good parents of our infancy. We find them in the employer and business associates who help provide us with our livelihood; in the wife or husband who gives us love, comfort and protection; in heroic leaders who inspire us with courage and faith. So, too, we find them in, the patient teachers and companionable friends who lift us out of ignorance and loneliness through their sympathetic understanding of our needs.

But there is another half to the story of our search for love. Although we always remain in part a child, we also grow up and become adults in our own right. Once we attain this status, other people inevitably look to us as replacements for the good parents of *their* infancy. We, too, are now expected to give help, sympathy and understanding —to provide others with a parent's love and protection. We are thus confronted with a hopeless stalemate unless we find a way to adjust our mutually opposing claims. If we are to establish satisfactory bonds of love with one another on a mature level, we must somehow manage to meet each other's requirements.

Only one solution can effectively hurdle the impasse. Each of us must accept the difficult task of playing a dual role in life. Each of us must acquire the subtle flexibility of heart that permits us to give and to receive at one and the same time—and to do both without hostility. A truly lovable person, in other words, can only be one who combines in himself the qualities of both a good child *and* a good parent!

If we look about us at those who are chronically unhappy and unloved, we will usually find that somewhere they have failed to meet this dual challenge. A basic error commonly made by such persons is to retain infantile hate as a characteristic pattern of reaction when life does not go exactly as they wish.

One of my patients a few years ago, for example, was a young man of twenty-five who had made a dismal failure of things because of such an approach to the world. He was in many ways a charming and attractive person, with a certain ability as a musician; but he had fallen into a completely irresponsible way of life. He considered work a form of slavery, lost one job after another largely because he resented the interference with his "freedom," and had no scruples about borrowing money from well-to-do relatives and friends to keep himself going.

The young man justified his Bohemian way of life on the grounds that he was an artist and could not be expected to conform to conventional standards. As we discovered, however, the unconscious motive for his behavior was a compulsive desire to make his family look after him. His parents had separated when he was a little boy, and he had grown up with the conviction that he had been deprived of his proper share of love. His irresponsible conduct was a form of hostility born of this resentment. Like an angry child, he used it as a weapon against his family and friends, compelling them to give him the kind of protective care ordinarily reserved for helpless infants.

Love or Perish

In time, of course, he exhausted the patience of his bene-factors. They began to reject his further appeals for assist-ance, until he was driven to living alone in a miserable basement room. There he eventually became ill for lack of proper food, and his parents had to come to his rescue. This had always been the young man's unconscious objective. It was a way of forcing his parents to pay what he con-sidered an unfulfilled debt. Fortunately, they were brought to understand the underlying nature of their son's dif-ficulties, and they arranged for the psychiatric help he needed to pull him out of his self-devised emotional trap.

Now, for most of us, life soon enough presents no choice but to outgrow such extreme states of dependency upon others. We usually learn to abandon our infantile patterns of behavior at least to the extent that we work at our jobs and provide for our own minimum needs. But many per-sons, while they manage to carry out these external duties, still maintain an inner emotional life of hostility very much like that of the dependent musician. They do their work grudgingly, with just enough competence to insure a bare economic foothold. They walk among their fellows with a secret envy of those who have more success. The inevitable frustrations of daily existence are viewed as a personal abuse, and they feel that the world owes them something beyond the circumscribed routine they so bitterly resent. At every opportunity they give vent to their suspicions and their grievances, and even wreak vengeance upon those who are too weak to oppose them.

Men speak to one another in the language of the uncon-scious where vital matters are concerned, and a basically

Lovability

hostile attitude of this kind is instantly perceived. It evokes immediate rejection, like that of a parent toward a "bad" child, and thus from the start destroys the subtle activity and interplay of the "good" emotions that are the very essence of love.

We must all take into account this fundamental psychological mechanism if we wish to make the most of our relationships with others. No outward artifice can conceal our inner hostilities once they exist. Neither should we deceive ourselves into thinking that we can simulate the easy, friendly outlook which denotes the "good" child who has learned in his unconscious to accept others on a basis of mutual accommodation. It is only when we genuinely bring such an attitude to everyday life that we can make an effective appeal to the "good parent" in other people, and thus spontaneously call forth the desired reaction of love, sympathy, generosity and co-operation.

I have already indicated that we do not fully complete the circle of love unless we advance further and also assume the role of the good parent. This is the capstone of maturity, and admittedly difficult to attain. It requires a boldness of spirit and a serenity of conscience, for it signifies that we, ourselves, have replaced *our own* parents—an act devoutly anticipated in childhood, yet long viewed with fear and guilt as the mark of the evil "usurper." One need not wonder that many of us shrink from taking this step forward. Unconsciously, we still retain memories of a time when it was actually forbidden, or when we may even have been punished for daring to assume the prerogatives of parents and grown-ups. The painful feelings associated with these early attempts at maturity tend to reappear with our later efforts in the same direction, and it is far from easy to shake them off.

That is why we usually make little headway when we condemn people for evading their responsibilities as adults. Their actions may seem to justify the accusation, but when we probe into their unconscious minds we are more likely to find that they would be only too glad to accept those tasks if they could. It is fear—not lack of responsibility— which most often holds them back. They avoid the duties of a good parent, paradoxically, because of inner anxieties aroused by the wish to fulfill precisely this role!

Yet, however normal such fears, we cannot forever take shelter behind them. Reality teaches us that all life, in a sense, is a trade; and in emotional matters, too, we cannot buy unless we also have something to sell. If we persist in holding on to the relatively passive role of a child—(even the "good" child)—we will have to remain content, at best, with the favors that others may see fit to bestow. When we do so, we limit the horizon of our activities to the range of our nearest benefactor, and not according to the talents we possess in our own right. Our destiny will then be to dwell among the anonymous and the unnoticed—safe, perhaps, but surely with little of the exhilaration that comes when we go forward courageously and hew our own path in life.

It is only when we ourselves act as good parents that we achieve man's most enduring victory—the power to initiate our own circle of love. When we offer help, sympathy and encouragement to others, we give them reason to forego their own hostilities and to come forward with support in return. We thus create a subtle exchange of love which feeds itself endlessly once it is set in motion. It then becomes a self-generating force that continually forges new bonds of love and causes our lives to expand into an ever-widening sphere of activity and communication. In this way we rise to our fullest stature as human beings, earn the loving admiration of our companions, and so move triumphantly into the company of leaders and heroes among mankind.

Self-Discovery, Faith, Love

Every person's emotional history is a delicate thread of individuality woven around the common spool of humanity. Although the need for love is universal in mankind, there is infinite variation in the sensitivity with which we respond either to its gratification or its denial. Everyone faces the task of curbing his aggressive impulses; but we differ constitutionally in the strength of our primitive drives, and for some of us the problem will always be less severe than for others. Fate, too, refuses to play its role twice in exactly the same way, so that even members of the same family often develop opposite traits of character and personality.

Nevertheless, in one significant respect we all share the same psychological destiny: All of us emerge from the period of childhood with a partially distorted view of life. As a corollary, adulthood confronts each of us with the same psychological obligation—we must all engage in a process

203

of self-discovery before we can correct these false views and achieve the ultimate victory of mature love.

Now there is a mistaken notion current that only those fortunate enough to escape conflict and frustration in childhood can ever hope for true happiness in later life. Such a view reveals a basic misunderstanding of modern psychiatric discoveries, as well as of the meaning of life itself. For childhood, by its very nature, compels all of us to misinterpret reality and to store up grievances that have no foundation in fact. It does not matter how fortunate may be the actual circumstances of our early years. Nature itself drives every child to be insatiable in its demands for love, to exaggerate every rebuff into a mortal injury, to respond with murderous hate when its will is opposed. These reactions, born of the child's lack of conscious knowledge and experience, inevitably leave a residue of unconscious resentment, fear and guilt. A childhood without such misconceptions would be, in fact, an abnormal phenomenon almost beyond imagination.

It is important to remember that every normal life must include conflicts, fears and anxieties. Adolescence and marriage, parenthood and middle age—each new phase brings new tensions and requires new adjustments. We do not become ill and unhappy because these everyday problems arise, but only when we fail to *solve* them satisfactorily. In the same way, the false views of childhood are a normal outcome of our early experience. They become stumblingblocks in later life only if we persist in holding on to them *as if* we were still children.

To hope for the elimination of conflict and frustration

Lovability

is a foolish fantasy which violates both scientific theory and common sense. Psychiatry has given us new insights into the *origin* of these problems that we may be better equipped to dispose of them when they occur. It has provided new tools and directives, that is, to aid us in the task of *coming to terms with reality*. This is a significant enough contribution—but the task itself has faced mankind from the dawn of history and will continue to do so at every turn along the path of life.

What are some of the directives offered by psychiatry to help us in this process of self-discovery and adjustment to reality? What are some of the steps we can take to release our energies in the fullest service of love?

Foremost among these, in my experience, are three which have virtually universal application. They are the following:

1. *We must forgive our parents for the injustices—both real and imaginary—we received in childhood.*

Who can look back with wisdom upon his early years and not concede that in many grievous ways he had failed to understand and judge his parents properly? Childhood is an age first of overemphasis and exaggeration, then of rash rebellion, and often later of casual indifference. All of us began by endowing our parents with godlike qualities both of good and evil. When they gave us love, we exalted them to the company of angels; when they ignored or punished us, we turned them into demons. As children, we could not know that our parents, too, may have been torn and harassed by the burdens of life; that others in the family may have had equal claim to share their strength; or that we ourselves may have demanded what was beyond their power to give. We expected infinite love and perfection of them, and we interpreted each lapse as a sign of injustice or treachery.

Every person's original image of his parents is thus based in part on a distortion of reality. The picture is overlaid with additional errors when, in our later bid for independence, we condemn all our parents' ways as wrong and outworn in order to justify our own new paths. It is natural enough for us to do so. But by the same token we accumulate a mass of grievances, resentments and hostilities of which only a small number, as a rule, have genuine validity.

Psychiatry teaches us that we must unburden ourselves of these false resentments if we are to become lovable and loving persons in our own right. For our attitude toward the world is modeled upon the inner image of our parents that we carry in our hearts, and our feelings toward other men and women are automatically governed by the love or hate which predominates in this inward vision of our fathers and mothers. If we stubbornly shroud the remembered portrait in the dark draperies of ancient grievances, we condemn ourselves to behave toward others like a disgruntled child who shuts himself off in a corner, where he wallows alone in gloomy self-pity and hurls malevolent glances of vengeance at his imagined oppressors.

Both wisdom and self-interest dictate that we come out of these shadows and stand in the tolerant light of maturity. Our normal course must be to identify with our parents, to see with their eyes, to suffer with them what was their own lot of hardship and trial—yes, and also the injustices they themselves in an earlier day may once have received. Then our childishly rigid "I accuse" will be withdrawn, and in its

Lovability

place will come the adult's tender "I understand." We will then be able to dwell with gratitude upon that measure of genuine love and care that our parents in reality bestowed upon us. In a spirit of forgiveness, we will see how little, after all, there was to forgive—and how much to be cherished!

Every distorted segment of the past that we bring into proper focus automatically makes our present vision more sharply attuned to reality. When we forgive our parents, we free ourselves of the neurotic need to demand "restitution" from the men and women who later replace them in our hearts. We no longer will expect the whole world to love us by way of compensation, nor will we retreat in sullen despair when signs of human frailty appear in those who do give us their love. We will learn, instead, to seek out the good and to preserve it with renewed tenacity. Thus our tolerant *inward* view will be reflected in *outward* benevolence, and thereby lead us to recapture the love we once deemed lost.

2. *We must have faith in a universal power greater than man's—the source of life and love.*

Of all human emotions, perhaps the most devastating is the feeling that one is alone in the world. The abandoned child, the ostracized member of a group, the rejected outcast of society—none is so desolate as the person who feels that he is isolated, unwanted, or without some relationship to any other living force in heaven or on earth. For if the essence of life is love, the essence of love is union; and no man can experience love who has no object outside himself with which he can join.

All of us spend our lives in a constant search for such an

object. We find it at first in the parent of our infancy, but as we grow up we transfer these feelings of love elsewhere. I have previously shown that in every phase of life we find a series of substitutes—in our work, in our social relationships, in the families we ourselves establish when we attain maturity. On a larger scale, society itself emphasizes the need for us to merge with outside groups, for it is through union with others that we "bind" our aggressions to love and thus bring them under control.

Yet experience teaches us that human bonds are fragile, and even the strongest of them may be snapped without warning by death, violence or the tyranny of fate. Moreover, mankind as a whole feels the need to ally itself with a beloved object, and it is here that we can all join together to hold a common faith in that force we call God, or the power which regulates the unfathomable workings of the universe.

In the name of religion, men have wrangled over creeds and fought over theologies, each convinced that his own is the one true revelation. All through history, too, different peoples have held different official concepts of God, and have even waged war to support their beliefs. Yet, underlying all these varieties of creeds and religions, one basic concept has always predominated. It is the view that there is a univeral power greater than that of man's, and that we must have faith in it as the one sure anchor that will support us throughout life.

Some find this manifestation of God in the infinite distances from star to star. Others see it in the eternal cycle of birth and death, of day and night, of summer and winter—

overwhelming phenomena all, and recurring endlessly de spite what individual man may do. Still others obtain their understanding of God through the teachings of their church, each according to his own convictions. But all are united in the realization that the vast universe, with its baffling multiplicity of miracles, is beyond mortal comprehension. St. Thomas Aquinas declared: "Every mind must face the rebuff of mystery." Even the wisest of men have always had to be content with but a fragment of the whole truth.

In the face of this mystery, we can overcome our ultimate loneliness only by a feeling that we are a part of the great design that controls the universe. We do this by transferring our love and faith to God, and thus achieving an inner security that transcends all human failings—the "peace of God that passeth all understanding." In my experience, it is through this faith that we obtain our most powerful sense of love, of receiving love, and of being at one with all humanity.

3. *We must accept our own aggressive impulses as a natural and normal part of life.*

It is not often that men are brave enough to peer into the secret labyrinth of human nature and remain unshaken by the dark spectacle they behold. "We all have feelings inside that would shame hell!" declared the gentle Robert Louis Stevenson with a poet's courage; yet for most of us the subterranean mind of man has in the past presented far too frightening a picture to bear any but the most timid scrutiny. In our unconscious lies all the primitive fury of the elements, all the fierceness of the jungle beasts, all the cruelty of the naked savage. Mankind has spent millenniums of patient effort to build a veneer of civilization around this primitive core, and one easily understands our universal reluctance to pry beneath the protective cover.

Civilized morality consists of the legal and ethical barriers erected against these primitive aggressions. Mankind has always required an authoritative voice of restraint to prevent the wild anarchy that would follow if the grosser crimes of murder, incest and cannibalism were left unchecked. We see the wise necessity for these proscriptions when our children in miniature repeat the historical evolution of the race. Every wise parent knows that at certain crucial junctures we must mark out the proper way of life with firm precept and command. That is how the child develops its moral conscience, its sense of justice and integrity, and hence its ability to win an acceptable place in society at large.

Yet too often we pay a severe price in individual unhappiness for the social law and order obtained in exchange. Some of this unhappiness is perhaps inevitable; but psychiatry reveals to us that much of it can be avoided. For in its zeal to impress its desirable precepts upon men, civilized morality has often unnecessarily denounced our aggressive drives as "evil," and insisted that we abandon them on pain of eternal punishment. By relegating these impulses to a criminal underworld of "sin," it has caused men to turn aside from their contemplation in shame and fright.

Men once had this attitude toward physical disease. They used magical threats and prohibitions to banish the "evil" spirits that afflicted their bodies—but the microbes did their deadly work nevertheless. I believe our moral evolution is

Lovability

rapidly reaching the point where we must face the psychic realities of human nature with the same calm objectivity we have learned to use in probing man's physical nature. To the tried and true morality of the past, in other words, we must now add a more mature *method* that will put its teachings into better effect.

Modern depth psychology has taught us this: Man's elemental drives do not vanish by themselves simply because we may ban them as "vicious" or "immoral." When we do not acknowledge to ourselves the existence of our own primitive impulses of aggression, we often develop a neurotic sense of guilt. To shake off this guilt, we unconsciously either punish ourselves with wasteful failure and illness, or we "project" our own emotions onto other persons and accuse *them* of the hostile feelings we ourselves bear in our own hearts. We thus use our aggressive energies to create imaginary enemies where none may exist, and so plunge ourselves into futile conflicts which can only end in destruction for all.

Mankind must learn to accept the psychological truth that *there is no inherently evil side to human nature*. We begin life simply with the energy derived from our primitive impulses of love and aggression. Every bit of this energy is potentially useful and valuable in itself. We must learn to study the nature of these forces within ourselves and look upon them with equanimity if we wish to obtain effective control over them. To recoil in fear from their elemental power is to become their victim instead of their master. The real "evil" comes when through willful ignorance we avoid the truth; the real "crime" occurs when we fail to use love

211

Love or Perish

as the guide which will direct these primitive energies to constructive ends; the real "immorality" is worked when we allow neurotic guilt to distort their useful power into destructive hate.

Admittedly, it will not be easy to accept self-discovery and self-control as the pathway to love where men have been accustomed to rely on external warning and authority. Yet the effort must be made, for we can never truly possess love unless we possess it of our own free will. The frightened, neurotically guilty man is a loveless man, however diligently he may obey the laws of good conduct. We now know, however, that our greatest fear is always of ourselves —but only of that which is *unknown* or *concealed* within ourselves.

Long ago the great poet Friedrich Schiller said: "There is no freedom but love." To this the voice of modern psychiatry may add: "There is no love but truth!" *Self-discovery, Faith, Truth*—through these we bring love into our lives, ourselves become lovable, and so reach out to forge with our fellow men the enduring bonds that preserve life.

GLOSSARY

NOTE: *Occasionally in this book I have made use of psychiatric terms for which no exact synonyms exist in everyday language. In each such instance, the terms are either self-explanatory or have been sufficiently defined in the text to make their meaning clear. Some readers may nevertheless find it of value to have a fuller discussion of these terms conveniently at hand, and I have added the following glossary with this in mind. I have not attempted to make my discussion exhaustive, but merely to give more background information about a fascinating field of human knowledge.*

—S. B.

aggression—All living beings have an impulse to destroy. This impulse is a basic instinctual force, according to psychoanalysis, and is called "aggression." Curiously enough, it can be directed outward toward others, and it may be turned inward upon oneself. In its primitive form, aggression is a means of self-defense. It may be also a means of self-destruction if it is not employed constructively. The act of converting aggression for useful social purposes requires that it combine or fuse with the love impulses. This is the act of *sublimating* (see below) aggression, one of the major tasks of the individual in civilized life.

anxiety—Anxiety is a form of fear. It is a state of painful uneasiness of the mind and is usually accompanied by physical symptoms of distress: rapid heartbeat, shallow breathing, rise in blood pressure, trembling and sweating, etc. Anxiety, like all fear, is one of the ways we defend ourselves against a condition we regard as dangerous.

However, there is a significant difference between anxiety and normal fear. Normal fear occurs when there is a real danger in the external world. Anxiety is a defense against our own unconscious, amoral impulses that violate our sense of right and wrong.

For example, a person may have a strong desire for the destruction of someone who continually gets in his way. Unconsciously, he is frightened by this primitive desire. He feels guilty about it and develops an anxiety reaction as a defense against it. In such cases, the person usually finds a plausible external reason to explain his anxiety. This may range from the possibility of losing one's job to the

213

Love or Perish

threat of a world war—but the real cause is always the reprehensible unconscious impulse.

ego—When we use the word *ego* in everyday life, we generally mean the self. In psychoanalytic use, the term refers to that part of the primitive mind—that of the newborn infant, for example—which has the function of dealing with the influences of the external world. It is the way station between the outside world and the unformed internal world of the primitive mind. The ego is thus a mental structure that grows from childhood on. One part of it faces the external world, where its function is to perceive and interpret reality. The other part faces inward toward the unconscious mind, which it seeks to protect and control. It adjusts both worlds to each other and keeps (or tries to) the peace between them.

In childhood the ego is still relatively feeble. It needs time before it can grow and organize itself into a mature structure. That is why love and encouragement are so important in the early years. Children need help and support—rather than harshness and severity—because their ego is not yet strong enough to control the primitive unconscious without outside assistance.

frustration—As used in this book, frustration means the denial of basic desires or needs. Frustration may result from external causes, or it may be self-imposed. The fate of older people in our society is an example of the former. Many older people suffer serious frustration because of the limited available outlets for

their instinctual needs. This is especially true of women whose husbands have died and whose grown children have left home. They no longer feel needed and have no vital interests on which they can expend their energy.

Self-imposed frustration, on the other hand, occurs when we check, or *inhibit*, the instinctual impulse while it is still in the unconscious, or before we are consciously aware of it. An *inhibition* restrains the impulse before it can emerge and come into conflict with one's moral judgment. Because of severe training or punishments in early childhood, for example, many people inhibit the impulse to look, and thus lose their sense of curiosity. A certain amount of inhibition is, of course, normal and necessary in civilized life, but too often it becomes a source of harmful frustration.

neurosis—A neurosis is, very simply, an emotional conflict, or an internal emotional battle. It occurs in the unconscious mind and we are generally aware of it consciously through such symptoms as anxiety, depression, fear of closed spaces, stuttering, or morbid fear of germs. *Neurotic* symptoms may range from mild to severe, and they are usually an exaggeration, or intensification, of what the so-called normal person may experience. All of us may stutter, for example, in times of embarrassment; and it is perfectly normal to have moments of anxiety during a severe crisis, or to experience fear if accidentally locked in a closet with no one around to come to our aid. But many persons grow alarmed when

214

reading about such symptoms and conclude erroneously that they are suffering from a neurosis. It is only when these reactions become unduly exaggerated into a regular pattern of behavior that one may infer the existence of a neurosis—namely, a deep-seated conflict which is responsible for these outward symptoms. Generally speaking, one's behavior is not neurotic unless it causes intolerable mental pain to oneself or prevents one from functioning effectively in life.

psyche—This word comes from the Greek and is the technical term for the mind. In psychoanalytical usage, however, a *psychic* process means more than what we ordinarily describe as mental activity or thought, for the psyche also includes the unconscious part of the mind. Theoretically, the psyche is assumed to be a separate organ or system that influences all parts of the body.

psychoanalysis—The science of psychoanalysis was defined by Sigmund Freud, its founder, as the discovery and study of the unconscious (the deep and hidden processes of mind) in mental life. The term is properly applied only to the body of theory and observation assembled by Freud and his followers. Freud has often been quoted, erroneously, as saying that all neuroses are caused by sexual conflicts. Actually, as he himself said, they are caused by one's inability to love and be loved.

Psychoanalysis is also the name of the method used by *psychoanalysts* to treat mental and emotional disorders. Briefly, this method employs "free association" and the analysis of dreams to discover the unconscious factors behind the patient's illness. By means of interpretations furnished by the *analyst* (a physician trained in the psychoanalytical method of treatment), the patient is slowly re-educated until he is able to face his unconscious impulses without fear and thus to turn his energies to constructive goals.

psychosis—*Psychosis* is the term applied to any of the severer types of mental disorder. *Psychotic* denotes extreme disorientation, with radical disruption of the normal adaptations to reality. It refers to those deranged mental states we ordinarily describe as "insane." The majority of the *psychoses* are usually grouped under the general headings of *schizophrenia* (see below) and *manic-depressive psychosis*, which is characterized by extreme depression alternating with periods of exaggerated vivacity and grandiose ideas.

psychotherapist—*Psychotherapy* is a general term and means the art of treating mental and emotional disorders. The *psychotherapist* may use one or more methods to effect a cure. These include suggestion, persuasion, psychoanalysis and re-education. Hypnotism was a method used in earlier days, and Freud himself employed it at the beginning of his career. But Freud abandoned hypnotic treatment because of its limitations and also because its curative effects were only temporary. In recent years modified forms of hypnotism have again come into use, especially as a method of rapid diagnosis.

reaction-formation—This is a psychoanalytical term which can

Love or Perish

be best defined by its operation in everyday life. Cruelty is natural to most of us when we are children. This cruelty is an unconscious, infantile tendency and we know full well that it is socially unacceptable. As we grow and mature, experience teaches us that we cannot give free rein to it, and we learn to develop the opposite quality of kindliness in its place. We therefore develop a conscious, socially positive attitude as the antithesis to our unconscious, negative attitude. Kindliness, in other words, is the *reaction-formation,* or defense, against one's own cruelty. All reaction-formations are developed through education and experience, and they are a basic part of social morality.

schizophrenia—This is a general term and refers to that class of mental disorders in which there is a more or less complete withdrawal from the world of reality. The *schizophrenic* person suffers from delusions and hallucinations. He may imagine that others are out to kill him or persecute him; or he may have grandiose fantasies in which he believes that he is God, or Napoleon, or the Redeemer.

sublimation—Sublimation is a modification of a primitive drive to meet an adult goal. Unlike a *reaction-formation* (see above), sublimation does not change the instinct and is not a defense against it. It merely deflects the primitive drive so that its mode of expression is modified, with a socially acceptable goal substituted for the original object. For example, most children take pleasure in displaying themselves in the nude.

Modesty (or its more extreme form, prudery) would be a *reaction-formation* against this normal infantile exhibitionism, whereas dancing, acting or speaking on the stage before an audience would be an adult *sublimation* of it. Sublimation is the most fruitful way of developing one's character and personality because it enables us to employ our primitive energies for socially useful purposes.

somatic—In biology, the Greek word *soma* is used to designate the organic tissues of the body. *Somatic* is thus a technical term with pretty much the same meaning as our everyday word "physical." Although it is used in contradistinction to *psychic* (see above), psychiatrists in recent years have come to believe that both *psychic* and *somatic* processes are harmonious, or complementary, elements of the total organism. This belief has given rise to "psychosomatic medicine," in which treatment is based on the premise that many organic illnesses have a *psychic,* or mental, aspect. Migraine headache, for example, is often traced to otherwise unexpressed emotions of rage in the unconscious.

transference—Psychoanalysts use the term *transference* to describe the process whereby a patient reproduces his early emotional attitudes of love and hate during the course of his treatment. The patient, in other words, again experiences the love or hate originally felt toward his parents and *transfers* this emotional attitude toward the analyst. Another way of describing this process is to say that the early repressed emotions

Glossary

toward the parent are *displaced* on to the analyst.

During psychoanalytic treatment, this is done with exaggerated intensity. But to a lesser degree *transference,* or *displacement,* occurs constantly in everyday life. Our psychic energies are mobile; and when one avenue of expression is for some reason blocked off, another may be substituted. That is why we can turn our love or hate from one person to another and from one idea to another. This *displacement* of our emotions is highly useful, but it can also be the source of confusion and misunderstanding in everyday relationships.

unconscious—The *unconscious,* as defined in psychoanalysis, is the buried part of the mind. It is the storehouse of our primitive drives, childhood impulses and forgotten memories. An unconscious mental process is one of which we are not directly aware, and usually we can trace its existence only through its effects. The behavior of hypnotized persons affords us a graphic demonstration of the way the unconscious works. A hypnotized subject, for example, may be ordered to open an umbrella in the room ten minutes after he is awakened from the trance. He will carry out this action automatically as commanded, but will have no conscious recollection whatsoever of the reason for doing so. In the same way, our everyday behavior has unconcious motives of whose existence we are ordinarily unaware.

ABOUT THE AUTHOR

Dr. Smiley Blanton was born in Unionville, Tennessee. He was educated at Vanderbilt University, where he was a classmate of Grantland Rice's. Graduate work in English at Harvard and acting in stock companies and summer stock led directly into a short teaching career at Cornell. He organized the Cornell Dramatic Club and taught speech and dramatics.

After four years he decided to study medicine. He got his M.D. from Cornell University Medical School in 1914. Dr. Blanton worked at Johns Hopkins, organized and directed mental-hygiene clinics and child-guidance clinics and, in 1929, made the decision to go to Vienna and be psychoanalyzed by Sigmund Freud.

Teacher, pioneer, director of clinics—and always the unrelenting student of human beings in trouble—at the age of forty-nine he became a practicing psychiatrist and psychoanalyst in New York City.

When, some years ago, Dr. Blanton met Norman Vincent Peale, they compared notes and found that they had the same general approach toward solving the emotional problems of human beings. They joined forces and established the American Foundation of Religion and Psychiatry. In this organization, Dr. Blanton is director of the clinic and Foundation and Dr. Peale is president and chairman of the board.

One of his great hobbies is golf. He drives the ball 200 yards off the tee. He writes his publishers that he has been scoring in the 80s. Considering that he is now seventy-four years old, we think this is quite wonderful.